Praise for *A Map Is Only One Story*

"This collection is a vital corrective to discussions of global migration that fail to acknowledge the humanity of migrants themselves." —*Publishers Weekly*

"Fierce and diverse, these essays tell personal stories that humanize immigration in unique, necessary ways. A provocatively intelligent collection." —*Kirkus Reviews*

"A vast, astute collection exploring questions of identity and belonging. *A Map Is Only One Story* is about margins, ideas of home, migration, and the violence of borders, but it's also so capacious that it's impossible to summarize. Candid and devastating." —R. O. KWON, author of *The Incendiaries*

"*A Map Is Only One Story* has a kaleidoscopic effect, breaking our image of the world with fixed borders and identities to create something new again and again. In this anthology, finding home is more than just a search for a place, but for a way to exist. Funny, poignant, and thought-provoking." —AKIL KUMARASAMY, author of *Half Gods*

"Moving and intimate. These disparate voices come into their power when they reach beyond the broken self toward something greater—love, kindness, family—even as homes are lost, pride shattered, identities remade." —DINA NAYERI, author of *The Ungrateful Refugee*

Praise for *Catapult* Magazine

"It's tricky to pinpoint, exactly, what *Catapult* means for me. A publisher is only ever defined by the people who run it, and working with some of the industry's kindest folks, and its most thoughtful folks, who are nonetheless among its most incisive, can do a funny thing to a writer: it shows you some of the many ways to be. As a storyteller, sure. But also as a person. Mainly as a person. And maybe that's what sets *Catapult* apart, and what will continue to set them apart: they champion people, in their messy, glorious, unending multitudes."

—BRYAN WASHINGTON, author of *Lot: Stories*

"Writing for *Catapult* changed the way I saw my craft, and how I saw myself as a writer. I'd never written for a publication that I would call 'literary,' and as a queer person of color, I considered the notion of ever inhabiting that word to be a lofty goal. But that's the magic of *Catapult*: in the process of being edited and published there, I saw my narratives in a new light, as worthwhile gems waiting to be polished. My first longform essay for *Catapult*, about La Llorona and my Chicano family's history, remains one of the pieces I'm proudest of in my career. It wouldn't have been possible without *Catapult*'s dedication to publishing challenging, bold works that defy easy categorization, opting for complexity and rogue prose over standard fare. In the stories it chooses to uplift, *Catapult* is changing the game, both for its writers and for the literary world we inhabit. I'm as eager to contribute again as I am to read what they put out next." —JOHN PAUL BRAMMER, author of *¡Hola Papi!*

"As writers, our careers are dependent on gatekeepers who decide what and whose writing is published and read. As writers, also, we ultimately decide to whom we submit our writing and where we will find the best support and audience for our work. Which places make us feel seen? Which publishers are highlighting unique voices? Which publishers are moving the needle on changing the landscape of writing? Which publishers are finding and supporting uninhibited, high-quality, riveting writing that screams of tenderness and heart? For me, that place is *Catapult*. I'm both an avid reader of *Catapult*, as well as a published author via *Catapult*. The editors there 'get it' and apply their skills with meticulous craft and unfettered heart. And it shows in the writing I read in the magazine and in their books; I walk away learning something I never expected to learn but realized I needed to learn each and every time. *Catapult*: what a sanctuary for writers and readers."

—CHRISTINE HYUNG-OAK LEE, author of
Tell Me Everything You Don't Remember

CATAPULT

New York

Twenty Writers on

A MAP

Immigration

IS ONLY

Family

ONE STORY

and the Meaning of Home

Edited by

NICOLE CHUNG

and

MENSAH DEMARY

ISBN: 978-1-948226-78-3

Cover design by Nicole Caputo
Book design by Wah-Ming Chang

Library of Congress Control Number: 2019944449

Printed in the United States of America
10 9 8 7 6 5 4 3

CONTENTS

INTRODUCTION

Since its launch five years ago, *Catapult* magazine has published a wide array of personal narratives from writers all over the world, in hopes of realizing a central tenet of the magazine's mission and Catapult's overall company vision: through writing that seeks to bridge rather than widen the rifts between people, literature can provide a pathway to greater empathy and understanding.

First led by founding editor in chief Yuka Igarashi, along with this anthology's co-editor Mensah Demary, *Catapult* magazine publishes standout literary fiction and nonfiction that honors the intimate bond between writer and reader, while also engaging with the broader culture in the way only a daily publication can. It can perhaps be best understood as a clear, ongoing expression of Catapult's values, as well as our commitment to writers at all stages of their careers. Key to the magazine's editorial identity is the challenge we issue to each of our writers, encouraging them to identify opportunities to ask themselves hard questions even as they interrogate and investigate the world.

In *A Map Is Only One Story*, the first published anthology of writing from *Catapult* magazine, writers reveal and explore the human side of immigration: Victoria Blanco relates how those with family in both El Paso and Ciudad Juárez experience life on the border. Nina Li Coomes recalls the heroines of Japanese animator Hayao Miyazaki and what they taught her about her bicultural identity. Nur Nasreen Ibrahim details her grandfather's crossing of the India–Pakistan border sixty years after Partition. Krystal A. Sital writes of how one's undocumented status in the United States can impact love and relationships. Porochista Khakpour describes the challenges in writing (and rewriting) Iranian America.

Migration is an experience that crosses borders and generations, and the writers in *A Map Is Only One Story* share an array of perspectives as immigrants, children of immigrants and refugees, people directly affected by immigration policy and how this country treats those who come here. While their stories are different, a truth they share is that immigration is not, ultimately, the story of laws or borders, but of *people*—of individuals, families, and communities. As one of our contributors, Jamila Osman, winner of the 2019 Brunel International African Poetry Prize, writes in her essay: "A map is only one story. It is not the most important story. The most important story is the one a people tell about themselves."

Through the power of personal narratives shared by both emerging and established writers, *A Map Is Only One Story* offers a new definition of home in the twenty-first century. While this is the first anthology of writing from *Catapult* magazine, it will not be our last. Our hope is that this ongoing series will introduce many readers to exciting and essential voices—urgent, necessary writing that will help us all better understand ourselves, our communities, and the world we live in.

NICOLE CHUNG *and*

MENSAH DEMARY,

EDITORS

A Map Is Only One Story

Why We Cross the Border

in El Paso

Victoria Blanco

On the river

When I was a child, in the late 1980s and '90s, my mom would drive our family across the border from my hometown of El Paso to Ciudad Juárez, where my Tío Beto and cousins live. To reach the Santa Fe International Bridge, one of the official crossing points between El Paso and Juárez, we drove down Paisano, a road that parallels the Rio Grande. I saw Juarense families lounging under umbrellas, and the mothers and fathers holding their children's hands as they waded ankle-deep into the fast-flowing water of the Rio Grande. On days when the waters flowed more calmly, I saw families floating on rafts made of tires tied together with rope.

I begged my mom to park the car along the side of the road. I wanted to call across the river to the Juarense children and ask them to send a raft over so that we could cross to the other side and walk to my tío's house. This was the reason I gave my mom for wanting to cross the river. I didn't yet have words to explain that crossing in the raft would save us from having our car searched by Mexican border officials once we crossed the bridge. These officials, then and now, try to stem the flow of arms into the country by conducting random searches at their immigration checkpoint. I felt dread when the stoplight on the Juárez side of the bridge turned red, signaling that we had to pull over so that an armed guard, usually a man, could approach my mom to ask her the purpose of our trip to Mexico. The guards opened our trunk, and sometimes asked me and my two brothers to get out of our seats so they could check underneath. I felt my shoulders tense as I watched my mom politely answer their questions. When I asked her if we could instead cross the river on a raft, she said no, and that she'd explain why when I was older.

A few miles upriver from Paisano, the Rio Grande serves as the divider between Texas and New Mexico. Locals call the neighborhood the Upper Valley, a name that seems to describe the five-bedroom stucco homes, the pecan orchards, and the cotton and alfalfa fields. Now, in my thirties, there are vineyards I like to visit. I sit on a terra-cotta patio, sipping local white wine beside a fluorescent green alfalfa field, the bare Franklin Mountains in the near distance. I was raised a few miles away, at the base of the mountains, the desert silent and hard beyond my backyard.

Even in the summer, when clouds block the sun every afternoon and release a rain dense and pelting, the desert's rainwater has never been enough to nourish the orchards, fields, and vineyards in southern New Mexico and El Paso. In 1916, when construction of New Mexico's Elephant Butte Dam was completed, U.S. farmers began diverting water from the Rio Grande for American crops. Irrigation canals extend from the river like veins. Today, as drought caused by climate change worsens and the Rio Grande flows less full, the irrigation canals empty the river before it reaches the U.S.-Mexico border, a few miles downriver.

I should have grasped the meaning of the change in water levels on a summer day in 1995, when my older brother Sergio's Boy Scout troop gathered without their parents' permission to swim in a part of the Rio Grande that runs through the Upper Valley. They chose one of the least trafficked overpasses that arches over the river and rejoiced for half an hour in the cool water, a group of teenage boys with nothing to do on a hot summer day. There was a sign nobody noticed. A boy named David, who used to push me around on his skateboard when I was very small, dove into the water from the riverbank. The water was too shallow, even though it shouldn't have been, not in the summer. Sergio remembers a friend running to the nearest corner store to call an ambulance, and the boys pulling David's body out of the water and trying to resuscitate him. They realized only when the paramedics arrived that David broke his neck in the shallow waters. I remember my brother sobbing in our mom's embrace, and my ghostlike sadness, tears I mimicked but didn't comprehend, because I hadn't yet learned that life gone never comes back.

Under the bridge

While walking across the Santa Fe International Bridge in the early '90s, my mom, abuelita, brothers, and I witnessed families rush across the Rio Grande. We heard a whistle, the signal from the coyote leading the people. We looked through the chain-link fence, down to the river. A few Border Patrol agents positioned themselves on the U.S. side, ready to stop the wall of people. I felt my mom's grip tighten around my hand as dozens of mothers, fathers, daughters, and sons surged across the Rio Grande, the water waist-high. Adults held children in their arms or carried them in rebozos across their backs. We watched as the Border Patrol agents caught and detained some people while dozens more ran past and disappeared into the streets of downtown El Paso.

Throughout the 1990s, these strategized crossings happened daily, no matter the water level. Crossings increased throughout the decade as Juárez received refugees from southern Mexico and Central America, most of them indigenous and mestizo farmers from villages whose crops perished from drought and who suffered political violence caused by U.S. Cold War policies. They arrived in Juárez because the passage of NAFTA, in 1994, saw dozens of maquiladoras, American-owned factories, open in Juárez, creating thousands of assembly-line jobs. The building of the maquiladoras coincided with widespread drought, crop failure, and a collapsing Mexican economy, and many believed job creation would help Mexico's poorest citizens, most of whom rely on subsistence farming, the informal economy, or a combination of both. Ciudad Juárez grew from a town of 500,000 to more than 2 million in less than a decade. But subsistence farmers and laborers who hoped the maquiladoras would provide a stable life discovered the wages were not enough to pay rent or feed their families in this expensive border city. The government failed to build enough subsidized houses for the incoming families, and many resorted to building cardboard house colonies—which the government has not replaced with subsidized housing, twenty years later—at the edge of the desert, with no access to the city's amenities.

Surging the Rio Grande was a tactic that allowed thousands of families to enter El Paso each day. Border Patrol agents always caught a few hundred people, but the people seeking refuge from violent governments and the consequences of climate change always outnumbered the agents. Operation Hold the Line, a Border Patrol initiative that upped reinforcement along the river between 1993 and 1995 to stop the surges, ultimately failed because the groups of crossers simply grew too big to stop.

Several of my tíos and tías left Juárez in the 1950s because they couldn't find work. They moved to California and East Texas, and my tíos provided for their families on the tips they earned as servers in restaurants and their hourly wages as taxi drivers. My abuelos moved to the farming community of Delicias, a place they saw as an opportunity to make a living in their country. Their farm became successful and they saved enough money to send their only child to medical school in Guadalajara. There, my mom met a man from the United States. They fell in love and married, and she eventually became a U.S. citizen. Even after my mom and her husband divorced, she remained in the country, choosing to settle in El Paso. She wanted to live within driving distance of her parents, who remained in Delicias, but make her life in the United States. I was born in El Paso. Even though she raised us to see ourselves as American, my mom made sure my brothers and I understood our story was connected to the people rushing the Rio Grande.

In the river

Families knew to avoid crossing in the summer, when the rains caused the river to flood low-lying land. Mexicans know this river as the Río Bravo, a name that warns of the river's dangerous undercurrent. But families often risked the river's strong undercurrent and flash floods. Crossers drowned in the Rio Grande, even in places where the water only came up to their knees. The undercurrent, more forceful than many predicted, knocked mothers and fathers and children off their feet. Some evenings, I looked up from my homework to see family pictures, school portraits, and snapshots on the local nightly news, the names printed in white letters at the bottom of the screen. I noticed children my own age, the gaps in their smiles where they lost a tooth, the little girls' hair neatly braided and the tiny gold studs in their ears.

Many of the bodies were pulled from slower waters near the International Bridge of the Americas, a couple miles downriver from downtown El Paso. The connectors between El Paso and Juárez are busy with border crossers throughout the day. But sometimes the bodies floated unnoticed under the bridges, past the parallel downtowns, the high-rises on one side and the vendor-filled streets on the other. The waters carried them through the quiet neighborhoods east of downtown. Ranch owners and Border Patrol agents often spotted bodies downriver, beyond the city limits, drifting through the desert.

The water levels in the Rio Grande changed dramatically in the early 2000s, when New Mexico and Texas agreed to hoard more rainwater behind southern New Mexico's Elephant Butte Dam. Drought was further diminishing the river's and reservoir's water levels, so New Mexico and Texas devised a plan to let the Rio Grande flow only during the spring and summer, when the sprouting fields in southern New Mexico and El Paso need hydration most. Because the Rio Grande begins in Colorado and flows through New Mexico and Texas, the United States has prerogative to control the river, even if it means stymying the Rio Grande once it touches Mexican soil. In 1906, the United States promised Mexico 60,000 feet of water a year from the Rio Grande in exchange for Mexico waiving claims to the Rio Grande above the town of Fort Quitman, Texas. Farmers in Juárez also relied on the Rio Grande to nourish their crops, but as the river began to dry, the United States broke the promises signed in a treaty.

Today, the dam releases only enough water—about one-third of what the Rio Grande should hold—to sustain American pecan orchards and fields. Then, in the winter, when a thin layer of snow covers the Chihuahua Desert, the dam withholds nearly all the water, leaving a 60-foot-wide trench through farm country.

As farming in Juárez became obsolete, the city relied almost exclusively on the maquiladoras. Indigenous and mestizo men and women, who once lived from the land, stand in assembly lines for double shifts, fitting a handle, a lid, a chip, a screw with the kind of precision that causes their necks and backs to strain.

Across the border

When I reached my teenage years, my mom warned me to never go near the border. She reminded me of David's death, of tensions between refugees and the Border Patrol, and of news reports about Juarense women murdered and found in the desert. All of this violence, she said, was related to the border. This is the year that I mark as a turning point in my family's relationship with the Rio Grande. My mom stopped speaking of the river and instead warned us about the border.

By then, my mom was struggling with Sergio's tendency to head across the border with his friends. After David's death, Sergio gave up swimming in the river and instead began crossing the border to visit the bars that didn't ID, causing our mom anguished nights as she prayed for his safe return. Late in my high school years, I began crossing too, often returning at four a.m. Despite the recent 9/11 attack and the increased scrutiny at the border, I downed cocktail after cocktail in Juárez bars. I accepted drinks in clear plastic cups from men, fluorescent concoctions that stained my lips and left a sickening aftertaste. Sometime after midnight, I walked down Avenida Juárez with my friends, the bouncers in front of clubs enticing us with cervezas two-for-one, no cover. Pounding music spilled onto the street and followed us all the way to the international bridge, strangely lit and silent except for the Customs and Border Protection agents asking their questions. At the immigration checkpoint, I tried to walk straight and say "American." I dared the CBP agents to restrain me—force me to take a breathalyzer and call my mom to pick me up. To the officers who asked if I had a boyfriend, I laughed and demurred. Each time the agent waved me past, I allowed myself to walk haphazardly, laughing and linking arms with my girlfriends.

The bars on Avenida Juárez exist to cater to U.S. citizens looking for the novelty of a wild night in Mexico. When I was in high school, many Juarense service industry workers relied on Americans to become hooked on the fantasy of partying in Mexico. Juarense bar and club owners looked at Americans with disdain, even as they advertised foam parties and ladies' nights in their clubs. I didn't see myself as one of the Americans who escaped to Juárez for wild nights. My history and experiences on the border run too deep for me to ever consider myself fully American. But to Juarenses who rely on tourist dollars and who risk their lives to reach El Paso, my drinking and disregard for the Border Patrol's power must have made me seem arrogant.

By the fence

I returned from college in 2006 to find miles of steel fence erected along Paisano Drive. President George W. Bush's Secure Fence Act commissioned 700 miles of an eighteen-foot steel border fence, designed to "make our borders more secure." He called this measure "an important step toward immigration reform." A tall fence today runs through my two cities, following the course of the Rio Grande, so that anyone driving along Paisano sees the river and our neighboring city through a thick steel mesh.

Many El Paso and Juarense families decried the Secure Fence Act, calling for bridges instead of walls, and an open border. Citizens on either side of the border argued that our people deserve to visit our families even if some of us don't have enough money to pay for the border visa. Congressman Sylvestre Reyes, who served twenty-six years as a Border Patrol agent in El Paso and designed Operation Hold the Line, voted against the Secure Fence Act because he had learned a barrier "doesn't come close" to addressing undocumented immigration. He had learned that refugees will arm themselves against Border Patrol agents, risk drowning in the Rio Grande, and walk the desert in 120-degree heat for a chance to provide for their families. My family, too, opposed the fence. El Paso and Juárez depend on each other economically, but even more important, families cross back and forth every day to visit one another. We knew the fence was a violence to our binational culture. We knew the fence would create a distance between us and our family in Juárez, when what we wanted was for all of us to live peacefully.

It's December 2017, and my husband and I are walking with our baby across the Zaragoza International Bridge from Juárez to El Paso. It's a bridge sitting near the edge of El Paso, close to the desert opening eastward, toward the major Texas cities. We're commuting from my in-laws' home, where we've spent a week, to meet my mom in El Paso.

As we climb to the apex, where the river sits dry directly below and a graffitied plaque declares the dividing line between countries, the stench of sewage fills my nose. I glance at my husband, who has pulled his hood over his head even though it's not cold, even though the desert sun flushes our faces turned pale after months of weak light in the northern state we've chosen to make our home. The stench is rising from the dry riverbed, and when I look over the bridge's wire fence I see the border's steel fence and drainpipes emptying into the river. When the river is dry, people descend the cement banks to drink and rest in the shade of the steel fence.

Here, far from the city center, families once waded across

the Rio Grande in search of a country that would treat them with dignity. But now the drought and dam have stopped the flow of the river. A steel fence has risen by its banks. The Border Patrol stands guard, ready to turn families away. The night is drowned by streetlights spreading across the desert.

A Map of Lost Things

Jamila Osman

When I was in the fourth grade in Portland, we spent three months studying the Chinook salmon, the Oregon state fish. Our unit culminated in a class field trip to a small creek off the Columbia River Gorge. At Eagle Creek, a small basin where the Columbia River runs into the Pacific, the Chinook salmon comes to spawn, having crossed thousands of miles of sea in a journey that takes many years. When the female salmon finds her way back to the same estuary of her birth, she will lay anywhere from 3,000 to 14,000 eggs before dying.

The estuary is where the river meets the sea. It is the collision of two worlds; it is where the new world meets the old world, where life crashes headfirst into death. Death is always the final act.

As we watched the salmon return to the estuaries they had left so many years ago, I was filled with a jealousy that hollowed out my chest. I envied the salmon and their bloated bodies, the way they shimmered under the water when the sun's rays caught against their scales. I have returned to this same creek many times as an adult, and I still feel the same sense of jealousy I felt at nine years old. I sit on the wet earth and hold my knees against my chest as I watch the salmon spawn.

On clear nights at the creek, the moon floats just over the surface of the water. The landscape is blurred and distorted, hazy and untrue in the mirror of the water. I look at the moon against the river and feel a hunger crest in me. The salmon return at the same time every year: haggard, gray, molten. I envy the certainty of their journey.

Sometimes I run into hikers and tourists as I walk the trail to the creek. *Where are you from?* They will inevitably ask me.

Portland?

I answer their question with a question of my own.

Portland?

My last syllable lifts its head in desire.

•

Nobody leaves home thinking they will never be able to return. I wonder what my parents would have taken with them when they left their home in Somalia in the late '80s. Who might they have made amends with, what old haunts would they have visited one last time if they knew they would never be back?

My parents ended up in Oregon, and by the time I was in middle school we had already lived in five different apartment complexes. When my teachers would ask me where I was from,

I would shrug. I had already learned that to be part of a diaspora was to live freely, to make no promises. In phone calls to faraway relatives my parents always swore they would return, but distance and time make liars of us all.

It was not that my family disliked Portland. We loved many things about the city—especially its spring days, warm and wet—but it was a cautious love. My parents had loved a place once before, and neither of them had ever fully recovered from the war that had leveled Somalia in the early '90s or its aftermath. How could they recover? War is not a cough, it is a cancer.

The Somali government officially collapsed in 1991. My parents, abroad at the time, found themselves unable to return. Newly married, my mother pregnant with me, they lived for a brief time in Canada. During their first winter in Edmonton, there was a devastating snowstorm. My mother had never seen snow before. Her lips and knuckles were always bleeding in the cold; everything in this new world was a small wound.

My father, previously a student, became a cabdriver in this new country. It didn't take him long before he no longer needed to use a map to take people to the places they needed to go: banks and doctor's appointments, hair salons and shopping malls. Soon he knew his way around Alberta so well that, if he didn't speak with an accent, one would have thought he was born and raised there. He knew which roads to take and which to avoid. He knew the fastest route to the airport, and where to find the back roads when the city closed around him like a fist.

My father always kept an atlas in the glove compartment of our family's minivan. Before road trips, he would pull it out and lay it flat on the dashboard, showing us where we were going. He would run a finger back and forth between small streets and major roads, rivers and borders. My younger sister, Ayan, and I would fight over who would get the privilege of unfolding the map for him. When it was my turn, I savored the crinkle of the parchment, and the slow blooming of the world in front of me.

Maps held a type of magic for my father. In our living room he would pull out world maps, drag a finger through an ocean, point to Saudi Arabia, and say, "This is where my mother is." Other times he would point to where his aunts and uncles and various cousins lived. Somalia, India, Denmark, Canada: hundreds and thousands of miles apart, but neighboring countries in his heart. My father knew how to get everywhere; it was what we always admired most about him. But even he who could name the capitals of countries all over the world could never figure out how to get back home.

•

After four years in Alberta, my parents arrived in Portland in 1996. They cobbled together a life, and gave birth to four more children. They did their best to raise us in a world they no longer recognized. Portland was nothing more than the city in which we lived until it became, suddenly and without warning, the city in which my sister died. The day after her funeral, my mother and I sat on the couch holding hands. "This was never supposed to be home," she said through her tears. "But Ayan is here. How can we ever leave?" We buried my sister and we put down roots.

Grief transforms the topography. On a map I can point to the intersection where the car accident took my sister's life, the street where the funeral home is located, the cemetery where she is buried. But a map doesn't show the blood pooling on the pavement, the glass scattered at the edge of the road, the skid marks, the acrid smell of burning rubber.

A map does not proclaim that the United States is Indian country, occupied land. On a map, someone can trace a finger from one Anglicized city name to another and forget these lands were and are known by other names. Maps are a polite fiction. They never tell the whole story. They don't mark important things, like graves or genocides.

Thirty years after the ousting of British and Italian colonial forces from Somalia, a civil war erupted. A volcano turning the country to ash. The northern region declared itself an autonomous state called Somaliland. *We are our own country*, they proclaimed as the war raged on. They drew the cloak of British borders tight around themselves.

When the colonists came, they committed our edges to paper; they tried to cage us with their borders. A country is impossible to contain; a people are impossible to boil to the silt of parchment. A map is only one story. It is not the most important story. The most important story is the one a people tell about themselves.

•

I visit Hargeisa, capital of Somaliland, for the first time in 2012. The northern region of Somalia had remained relatively stable and peaceful since the mid-'90s, even as the southern region was besieged by Al-Shabab and U.S. drone strikes.

I imagine my parents' first airplane ride, their racing hearts and quick breathing. Maybe they dug their fingers into their thighs, their nails marking half-moons on their skin. I am not the first to cross an ocean in search of something elusive and intangible. I think of the war and the period of mass exodus when everyone who was able to flee the country left. Only those who were too poor or too old or too full of hope stayed behind. Hope makes children of us all, foolish, and reckless, and devout.

Hargeisa is not what I expect it will be, but the things we wait the longest for seldom are. The city is dry and the air crackles. The dirt is fine and coats clothes and skin. The trees are scraggly and flimsy. Everywhere I look there are buildings collapsing in on themselves, piles of concrete and empty houses.

Hargeisa is the city of my mother's birth, the city where my grandmother cut her teeth on the rough realities of womanhood. My grandmother, who lived with us for a few years in Portland before moving back home because she missed it so much, shows me around the city. She is embarrassed by the men in FC Barcelona shirts and the way they shuffle, dragging donkeys down dirt roads, hustling lukewarm water in enormous canteens. She is embarrassed by the piles of trash that stink in the blazing heat of a Hargeisa afternoon. It is an embarrassment that is tempered by her love for this place.

Even here in the land of my ancestors, I wear my foreignness like an ill-fitting dress. When I go to the market with my grandmother, shopkeepers leer at me and call me "the American girl." I wonder what part of my body has betrayed me. I wonder in what way I am branded. They wink at me and wave their products in my face: *Spend your American dollars here!*

Somalis call those of us who return to visit dhaqan-celis. It is a story in two parts: *dhaqan* means culture; *celis* is a return. We are a roving tribe of wanderers, scattered siblings, lost youth, reluctant expatriates, victims of impossible and auspicious circumstances. Everyone looks at us like we are lost. They ask us what we have come to find. We have no answers.

A body always returns to the place that shaped it.

A body always returns to its ghosts.

•

For years, scientists have speculated as to how salmon find their way back to their natal streams. One widely accepted hypothesis states that when salmon are young, they imprint the pattern of Earth's magnetic field where they are born. Years later, this memory serves as an internal GPS.

The last stretch of a salmon's journey is the most dangerous. The closer it gets to home, the more perilous the trek becomes. Sailors used to call salmon the leaping fish. They launch their bodies over entire waterfalls, and sometimes land directly in the mouths of waiting bears.

Today the Chinook salmon is on the endangered species list. Fluctuating sea temperatures, man-made dams, and declining water levels make the journey home nearly impossible. Every spring, fish biologists report increasingly high numbers of salmon carcasses in local rivers. According to a study conducted by scientists from the National Oceanic and Atmospheric Administration, Oregon salmon are slowly being pushed north toward Alaska as a direct result of climate change. As ocean temperatures continue to rise, salmon will seek out waters that better mirror the conditions to which they're adapted. In time, some species of salmon may disappear completely from the Pacific Northwest.

•

In the summer of 2015, one year after my sister's death, my parents, my four siblings, and I take a trip back to Edmonton, Alberta. Canada is our shared ground zero, my family's original sin. My father has made the trip enough times that he has committed the route to memory. There is no need to consult a map. I now wonder if maps have lost their magic for him; if he, too, has recognized that the places to which we are most desperate to return might not exist at all.

Driving south on US-95 we come to a small stretch of unincorporated land between the United States and Canada. I ask my father to pull over, and I get out of the car. I cry on the side of the road. I am mourning my sister, our shared childhood, the unfamiliarity of the world that now beckons me forward. One foot in Canada, one in the United States, I am a woman like the women before me, legs spread indecently, straddling worlds, caught between cities and countries and continents.

On that strip of land between the two countries, I realize I have always belonged everywhere at once: on the road; in liminal spaces; in the disputed territory between Somalia and Ethiopia where my father spent the ragged days of his youth. I have always belonged at the beginning of the world, and where it seems to end, where the sky meets the sea, where the sea meets the land, on a plane where the two become indistinguishable from each other and you can no longer tell if you are going home or leaving it.

Where are you from? People still ask me, but the answer is not simple. I am from a place beyond the scope of any map or road atlas. I am from a house of borrowed things, a land of irreconcilable and devastating losses, a terrain marked by grief. I am from nomads who moved in search of water, carving a home wherever they ended up, like water carves its shape into rock. I am from a wild hope, a blinding courage, a blur and madness uncharted by any cartographer. I am from a land unmapped and entirely my own.

•

When I visit Somaliland for the first time, I stay long enough to imagine I will be there forever. Friends from Portland call me and ask me when I will return home. Their questions jar me. As I pack to leave, my grandmother asks me to stay with her. I tell her I will return soon. We are always making promises we cannot keep. Go or stay, either way, something is lost.

Home is not an answer to a question. It is my grandmother's front porch where I first saw how dark the night was supposed to be. It is the swimming pool in our first apartment complex in Portland, where I learned to see without looking, underwater with my eyes closed like the mermaid I knew I was. It is the spot where my sister is buried. It is Eagle Creek, where the salmon spawn and then die, using their last reserve of energy to protect their eggs. The journey home is arduous. Surviving costs something. Returning costs something more.

Will I return to the creek when the Chinook salmon no longer swim in these too-warm waters? These days the creek fills me with sadness, as fewer and fewer salmon survive the journey each year. The world is changing, and I am trying not to be leveled by it. I am trying to find my place in it.

A part of me will always be the girl who watched the salmon return, even when there comes a day when they do not. Where my sister used to be there is only her memory. Soon, where the salmon used to spawn, there will only be their ghosts. To love a thing is to steel yourself against its eventual absence. I am learning to mourn a thing before it is lost.

•

Two months after I get my driver's license, my parents finally let me drive to my friend Sarah's house alone. She doesn't live far away, and I won't need to take a highway to get there. It is winter and it gets dark early. I promise them I'll be home before the sun sets.

On my way home, I take a wrong turn. I do not realize it until I find myself in a part of Portland I do not recognize. At night the city is strange and unfamiliar, cloaked in its own uncertainty. The fog swallows what little light my car pitches against the dark. I look around for a landmark, a bread crumb, anything that will lead me home, but I find nothing. I am always getting lost. I think it is because I have no point of reference. My heart can't spin itself like a top and tell me what direction to go in.

I am sixteen and easily roused to panic. I call my father. I put him on speaker and leave the phone on my lap as I continue to take wrong turn after wrong turn. My grip on the steering wheel tightens. I begin to cry as soon as I hear his voice. I am stuttering and my words tumble over one another in their haste to get out of my mouth. I hear my mother in the background: "Is she crying?" "What happened?" "Is she okay?" I hear her decibel level rising with each question.

My father has always been the calm to my mother's wild panic. "Are you driving?" he asks me. "Pull over."

I pull into the parking lot of an abandoned building. I tell him I am lost. He asks me for the name of the street I am on, and then instructs me to wait in my car with the doors locked.

I do as he asks, and eventually he pulls up beside me in the bat-tered white minivan we have had for way too long. I roll down my window and snivel.

"Follow me," he says, and I do. I follow him all the way home.

My Indian Passport

Is a Bitch

Deepti Kapoor

I read an interview with the author Lawrence Osborne, an expat Englishman pitched as an heir to Graham Greene. Osborne lives in Bangkok, and I was in Chiang Mai, in northern Thailand, at the time. He said, "This part of the world is full of escapees." I thought: "It's true!"

Osborne went to Thailand for the cheap dentistry but stayed for the quality of life. It helped that one *New York Times* article sustained body and soul for six months. In the interview, he spoke of his peripatetic existence, years of wandering and scraping by, not caring about money as much as experience. The only thing he really needed, aside from that money, was his passport.

But I'm Indian, so my passport is a bitch.

Access to the Various Countries of the World Is Not Available to All Human Beings Equally

Even when a visa is possible, it's far from simple. My country is materially wealthy, and has around 200,000 dollar millionaires, but it also has 180 million people living in poverty. Aspirational Indians, mainly from the vast demographic existing between these two extremes, have been eager to get out over the years, to make their way in the world, any way they can.

Because of this (and also the way many go about their exit), other countries are wary. As a matter of course, for a tourist visa application to even approach success, I need to present bank statements, letters of recommendation and introduction, return tickets, hotel bookings, proof of employment, and tax records. I have to convince the relevant official, beyond all reasonable doubt, that I'm planning on going home at the end of my stay.

As a writer, my income is not regular, I don't have a place of work; I don't have a two-week holiday block; I don't even have a regular working day. I don't have a safety net. I have a certain amount of fear all the time, but I crave my independence, too. I only wish, like Osborne, I could trade the insecurity for freedom of movement.

The Visa Run

Now picture this: I'm sitting at the Thai visa center in Vientiane, the capital of Laos. It's one of those outdoor courtyard setups, a corrugated plastic roof that changes color with the burning sun, rows of plastic chairs connected horizontally at the base, marked by the pen graffiti of the bored, and there's always one that's broken, which bends way too far back. We move in a slow line, a silent game of musical chairs. There are about a hundred people here. They are almost all white. Western travelers and expats. I eavesdrop on their stories of hardship, what they have to go through just to keep on staying in Thailand. Sometimes they have to wait *three whole hours* when they apply for the new visa. Sometimes they *don't have access to a photocopier* inside the center and have to pay for the one outside. Sometimes the officials *don't smile at them.* Every year, *the price goes up.* Occasionally I detect a sense of disbelief that they have to do a visa run at all.

I might blend in with these people on the surface, but they are nothing like me. Though I sit patiently, I want to shake them, say: Do you know how lucky you are? How virtue is bestowed upon you by your birth, by the land that owns you? Do you see that you can dress in rags while I must watch how I present myself at all times, knowing what the sight of my passport will do? I want to ask: How many Indian backpackers have you met? Not students, not immigrants, but backpackers, freely exploring the world? Do you realize how the world belongs to you? Do you know how long other people have to wait for something as simple as a passport?

We move slowly toward the window. Glue sticks, scissors, pens, folders of documents. My visa application is about to be rejected.

First World Problems

But why am I even queuing here, in this old French colonial city? First world problems, you see. I didn't want to spend another season at home in Goa trying to write a novel while friends, relatives, and acquaintances arrived on holiday, expecting to be entertained. Also, my paperback was coming out in the United States, and my brother in Hong Kong had a son I hadn't yet seen.

To kill several birds with one stone, my husband and I decided to spend six months on the road. I found reasonable tickets and a friend to cat-sit our apartment. We worked out an itinerary: first Hong Kong and then San Francisco and New York, where we would stay with family and friends. At the end of it, an impulsive plan to spend three months in Chiang Mai in Thailand, writing.

I got my U.S. visa in Delhi first, before we left. It turned out to be the easiest one. The officer looked at me, heard me speak, shuffled through my overabundance of papers, saw that I was already married and that I paid taxes in the States because of my novel, and had even had my novel reviewed in *The New York Times*. This gave me ten years. (I did watch applicant after applicant get rejected while I waited, though.)

But when I tried to get a Thai visa in Delhi, they said I could only get it within thirty days of arrival in Thailand, and that I should therefore get it in New York. Dissolve to New York, two months later: A stern Thai official is telling me I cannot get a visa here as an Indian because I am not resident in America; I have to go back to India to apply for it.

"But they told me—" I plead.

He shrugs.

"But I already have a ticket from New York to Bangkok!"

Not his problem. "Go back to India," he says.

Meanwhile, my English husband is politely handed an application form because he can get his Thai visa from anywhere.

Research on my iPhone, walking the Upper East Side, trying to find somewhere to pee, tells me my options: I can still get a fifteen-day visa on arrival in Thailand as long as I show hotel bookings and return tickets and sufficient money in my bank account. But this is problematic. Our Airbnb booking in Chiang Mai is for a two-month duration, betraying our intention of staying longer than fifteen days. More damning, we have no return ticket.

Our remaining weeks in New York are cloudy. What will happen when we try to fly? Even if I manage to get a fifteen-day visa, what then?

Interlude at the Airport

Because airlines are responsible for returning visa-rejected arrivals to their port of departure, they often behave as preemptive immigration officials. Mindful of the bottom line, they can act more zealous than the real ones. Even when we left India, the young Indian guy at the Singapore Airlines check-in counter scrutinized my ticket to Hong Kong and finally demanded to see my return ticket. I said there wasn't one; we were flying from Hong Kong to San Francisco. He demanded to see the return ticket from the United States. I said there wasn't one. "Well, show me your return ticket to India?" he said.

I didn't have one. "Is that against the law?" I asked.

He went through my passport, examining all my visas, flicking backward and forward through the pages for a long time, finally demanding to know what I did for a living, why I was traveling to Hong Kong, why I was traveling to the United States, why I was away from India for so long. He demanded to know when I would return. I said I didn't know. He was greatly disturbed by this, offended, even. He continued pressing me, until one of his seniors had to step in. "This is none of your business," the supervisor told the young airline official.

The Plan, and How the Plan Panned Out

In the weeks between my rejection at the Thai visa office in Manhattan and our departure from JFK, I came up with a plan: get into Thailand on the fifteen-day visa, dump our stuff in Chiang Mai, then go to Laos or Cambodia ASAP, and obtain a long-term visa there. All the backpacker websites and message boards explained how easy it was; they gave step-by-step guides. There was even a "visa express": a bus that took you on an overnight journey and deposited you directly at the visa office in Vientiane. First I had to get into Thailand, though, which meant I still needed to show a ticket out of Thailand within the fifteen-day visa period.

There's a certain Indian airline that allows free cancellation of a ticket within twenty-four hours of purchase, highly prized in situations like this. From this airline I bought a ticket to India on a date within the fifteen days. I printed it out, and immediately canceled it. It was this canceled but printed ticket that I presented to the airline at check-in, and which I intended to present to immigration at Bangkok.

But the check-in guy at JFK had a really long look at it, and for a while I thought he was going to enter it into the system and uncover my deception. This terrified me, made me frightened for what I would face upon arrival in Bangkok, and so at the layover in Singapore, I bought *another* ticket back to India and printed it out in the business center, knowing, now that the New York–Singapore leg was over, I could present this real ticket to immigration in Bangkok and still have the time to cancel it afterward in the airport without incurring a penalty.

Once in Thailand with my fifteen-day visa, I turned my attention not to writing, but to the visa run to Vientiane. I looked again at the numerous websites explaining how to go about it, how easy it was. But wait a minute . . . was it easy for *Indians*? It occurred to me they'd all been written with Western backpackers in mind. I contacted the owner of one of the most comprehensive and knowledgeable sites, and tried to get specific information about Indian passport holders. He confessed he had no idea.

We went to Laos (visa on arrival) anyway. We stayed in a colonial hotel. We drank good coffee in the morning and salt fish and beer at night. The next day we went to the Thai visa office, queued up on those chairs, listened to the complaints and woes of the backpackers, watched as they submitted their applications, watched as I was told, just like in New York, that Indians couldn't apply here, that they couldn't apply anywhere but from India. I would have to go back to Thailand and work it out from there.

A few days later, in a dingy office at the border of Laos and Thailand, I got another fifteen-day visa, standing alongside a wealthy-looking Chinese lady. And, after fifteen days, utterly defeated, I flew back to India on yet another ticket to get my visa, leaving my husband to wait in our rented Airbnb in Chiang Mai.

Exodus

As this insignificant little drama of mine played out, hundreds of thousands of humans with arms and legs and eyes and teeth and memories were fleeing Syria, Afghanistan, and Iraq. I watched them on CNN in one of the lounges in Singapore as I headed back to India, refugees heading for Europe, packing their bags and taking off, families carrying whatever they could, photo albums, falafel makers, cats, people clinging to their passports, fleeing ISIL and Assad and civil war and drone-struck towns and borders that are blown into dust, nation-states that have crumbled, which have been toppled, reshaped indefinitely, in barbarism, rape, slavery, torture—the casualties of hatred, ideology, lies, deception, ambition, calculation, and expediency. I watched the TV back in Delhi. A shelled city; Homs before and after. Buildings and corpses look one and the same, riddled with bullet holes, unclaimed. The living keep on because they have to.

Humans in an exodus: trudging, lurching, flinging themselves toward the European Union, drowning in the sea, living in tents, in the woods, in shelters, in strange cities far away, on the edge, neither here nor there, but desperate to live all the same. Paperless, homeless, failed by institutions, by leaders, by neighbors. Clinging to humanity all the same.

Later, I woke up in another hotel bed, in a cabin in the Himalayas, listening to the call of peacocks and a distant train that winds its way across the mountains. I switched on Al-Jazeera and made coffee. "It's not fair," a well-spoken, photogenic Syrian boy said in excellent English, living in a makeshift camp at the Greek border with Macedonia, teeming with disease, ankle-deep in mud. "If only they could feel what we feel."

Gap Year

Sometimes it seems to me a miracle that so many worlds exist on the same planet and don't collapse into one another and collapse. How do we do it? Even more so in the age of social media, where everything exists all of the time. How can I lie in that hotel bed, the pillow fluffy and white, and see this happen, and not only not fall apart, but thrive, make my coffee, walk along a trail, sit in a meadow and revel in the glory of nature?

From gapyear.com: "The more adventurous still often find themselves in South Asia, in countries like India, which is a great place for volunteering placements, and Nepal, popular for adventure travel like trekking."

It's amusing and frustrating to read about your country in such a way. India has always been a projection of the fantastical and unorthodox and wayward and spiritual. India as the physical site for the West's psychic lack, the irrational mirror. Concomitant: the plundering of India by the East India Company, by the British Empire, by Californian yogis. Here's the deal: We'll take your treasures and dignity and wealth and knowledge and curse you with holiness in return. India is the place to come find yourself. One of those places to visit in order to develop character or realize how lucky, generous, compassionate, brave, and open-minded you are, before you go back and get a job in the real world.

Signal

In 2014 the VII Photo Agency founder John Stanmeyer, working for *National Geographic*, won World Press Photo of the Year for his shot "Signal," depicting African migrants on the shore of Djibouti City trying to catch a phone signal from neighboring Somalia. On the visa run in Laos we did the same, standing on the deep sandy banks of the Mekong while local boys played football, using our Thai SIMs to try and catch the signal over the border at Nong Khai (and checking Facebook when we did).

This photo has stayed with me, arriving in odd moments and reentering my mind during early coverage of the Syrian refugee crisis. So many photos of refugees with their phones, taking photos, checking for a signal, trying to stay in touch with loved ones (sometimes on Facebook).

Around the time, *The Washington Post* published an article called "The Black Route," which detailed one family's journey from Aleppo, Syria, to Austria. The Samsung smartphone of Ahmed, the father, featured heavily; the former deliveryman had plotted their entire route on GPS. They also used it to take photos, to document their journey. There's one photo of Ahmed with Mostafa, his brother-in-law, on the beach at Ti-los, a Greek island off the coast of Turkey.

On Quora I found this question:

> Why is it that Syrian refugees can afford high-end smart-phones to take selfies, while I, as a Canadian, can't?

> Well, I probably could, but its [*sic*] hardly a priority when it comes to my disposable income.

As I wished the travelers at the Thai visa center in Vientiane could understand what it was like to have to explain myself everywhere I went, to have my country treated as a kind of playground, a testing ground, a baptism by fire, I suspected I would never understand what it is to be a refugee, without home, country, safety, possessions, tired all the time.

One should never say never. My own grandmother fled Pakistan during the Partition of India and Pakistan, witnessing atrocities on all sides, narrowly escaping, through the bravery of others, with her life. Her previously genteel world there was destroyed overnight. Violence comes from all sides, at any moment. No land is secure, and no border truly stable. History creeps, and it breaks.

Anecdote with Camels

Last year, my husband and I traveled to Ladakh, the northernmost region of India, whose capital city, Leh, was once an important station on the Silk Road. The trading routes came through Xinxiang into the Nubra Valley, over the 18,000-foot mountain pass Khardung La, and down to Leh. When the Red Army sealed the Chinese border after the Communist Revolution, some of the Silk Road traders were stranded in India. And some of the traders abandoned their camels. The descendents of those camels live on sadly in the Nubra Valley, exiled in the high-altitude dunes of Hunder and Sumer.

On that trip we also traveled to Turtuk, five kilometers from the Line of Control between India and Pakistan. Sometimes described as the last village in India, Turtuk was part of

Pakistan until the First Indo-Pak war, in 1971. Then it changed hands. Villagers went to sleep in Pakistan and woke up in India. Fathers were on one side, mothers on the other, husbands, wives, children, divided.

Until 2009 the region was completely off-limits, and until as late as 2014 even Indian nationals needed a permit to visit. Tourists could travel only as far as Hunder, where the sad camels reside. But a relaxation of the tourist rules has seen the region open up. We traveled in a shared taxi, the lunar, mind-zapping, Buddhist landscape of Ladakh changing as we moved westward, the wide valley narrowing until we were driving along the boulder-strewn road of a tight gorge. We wound this way and that, crossing over roaring water, dodging the sites of landslides, passing army checkpoints where our documents were checked and rechecked. Five hours on this road, squeezed into a taxi with seven other people, until we saw Turtuk ahead, a mountain oasis of fabulous cultivated land surrounding a river pouring down from above. The guesthouse we thought we'd stay in was being renovated, but its owner, a policeman, a big man in town, took us around until we found another place. For the next five days we wandered the village, played with the children in the fields, talked with the villagers, interviewed the zamindar, the old landowner from the historical ruling class, now living in pale destitution and obscurity with his ancestor's seventeenth-century sword. One day, we walked to the final army checkpoint before the Line of Control, gazed into the distance of Pakistan. It looked just like India.

A Note on Carpets

I've recently made a new acquaintance called Altaf, a Kashmiri gentleman, a dealer in antique and semi-antique carpets. I've always been interested in antique carpets, not only the carpets themselves, but the idea of selling them, of being in business, of moving a product. A product such as an antique carpet seems noble, challenging, a synthesis of commerce, art, and practicality. Knowing one can't make a living from being a writer these days, I've toyed with other revenue streams. One is teaching yoga, which I've done for five years. Another might be selling carpets. Selling stories of origin, the harshness and beauty of the landscapes from which the rugs are made, the sense of danger. Talking of the warp and the weft, the type of dye used. Casting my new enthusiasm here and there, it became apparent that people were most interested in rugs from Afghanistan and Iran. From the tribal regions. From war-torn lands. From inaccessible places. This rug in my sunlit living room has traveled from a place I cannot and will not enter, but it is here, telling a story.

Home

After five months and several thousand dollars' worth of wandering, we flew home. Our first night back, I sat at my mother's table and listened to the gossip. The interesting stuff, as always, came from her domestic, Rajesh. Like those refugees, like those migrants on the shores, he too clings to his smartphone. He sends her WhatsApp messages with photo greeting cards he designs himself, to which, for the sake of boundaries, she never responds.

Tonight he urgently recounts tales from his impoverished Bihar village. This time there was a scandal involving a boy and his sister-in-law, both underage, who were in love and ran away. A friend of theirs promised to lend enough money to get them to the nearest city—either Kolkata or Delhi—to find any work. But something went wrong at the decisive moment. As they left the village for their new world, the friend had no money to spare. So the young couple, chastened, doomed, had no choice but to return. They were separated on arrival and beaten mercilessly for their transgression, and their families were each ordered, by the village council, to pay a hefty fine, compensation for the lost honor. I asked Rajesh how much money they needed in order to start their new life: It was nothing more than twenty American dollars.

THIS HELL NOT MINE

Kenechi Uzor

The thing with hell is that often it is not. When its fumes are your air and its flames the light you see by, hell is the existence, your everything that is and could be. You become such a part of the inferno that you no longer see it, feel it—it becomes subliminal. In this hell one boils, like a toad in a cauldron, oblivious to the end. Except if the have-beens get to you. They are the escaped chinks of light who have been out to other realms, have seen better things, better promises, but now are back with tall tales of other hells closer to heaven, sowing questions. Misery results from listening to them.

We were the shackled miserables in Plato's cave. Because there was no difference to know, we abided our chains and shadows, confident and moored in our illusions. With the have-beens came knowledge and possibilities of doubt, and pain. And as our existence became branded, our air became fumes and our light scorching flames.

Down there and farther back in the Nigerian hell, the seeds the have-beens planted did what seeds do and on their tendrils

I clung till they grew me out of our hell and into the searing, naked light that is America. And the light burned through me in waves of depression: How could we not have known that our hell had wheels too and could have been moved up the rail toward heaven?

America, at first, did not look like hell. Its heat was subtle and creeping and polite with smiley pretensions, and its light a dazzling distraction, inoculating all to an indifference toward demise. But it was outside and ahead of Nigeria, which is what heaven always is to the inhabitants of lower hells.

I lived in Lagos, a haven of have-beens and once-weres, of pockets of light that give claws to darkness and red eyes to gloom. To live in Lagos is to want, forever grasping, groping for opportunities that blink away; a city of near-misses that keep you trying, reaching, harpooned by hope. Lagos is a tease. Hope is its curse. The aroma of food to the famished who cannot feed.

I'd had enough. I and others, we'd had enough.

So we sought escape, convinced that to leave was to live. We fled for dry eyes, for a sigh, for firm handshakes and raised heads, for two closed eyelids. We fled for our babies and grannies. For light. We fled for those we left behind. In search of a better country whose builder and maker was God.

Millions now we are, half dead: trekking through the desert, on foot through Morocco, Libya, on congested floats across the Strait of Gibraltar to Spain, the Strait of Sicily to Italy, to jails and through refugee camps.

And all for this?

•

I'd never needed pills to pull the shade, nor lacked excuses to want to live. I had no doctor in Nigeria. My doctor in America said many informed things. Nice dude. But I wished my money back. Adults with responsibilities seldom wake up at dawn adorned with joy. I am fine. I guess I am fine.

But America kicked harder with those questions that open archways to depression: meaning of life; now what and what next; thoughts of time missing by; of luck and determinism; the pointlessness of all things; doomsday. What's so wrong with suicide? We wrote on this and forgot in philosophy classes at the University of Benin. At first, I thought it was a change-of-scene syndrome that would pass. Then I was sure it was a depression caused by the twilight of America clashing against my home country. The offending news bites I thought would be easy to nix: mute, block, unfollow, unsubscribe.

The obscenity of humanity is that we often seek heaven to find hell.

It is impossible to avoid the flames of America. In this new hell were more unique pains than Nigerian demons could ever conjure. In America, apocalypse ticked minutes away. Here, suicide, homicide, and wrong sides blindside millions. Misery climbed out of the news to hug you close: My friend's nine-year-old, normal kid, shot himself and left a note; one minute we were playing *Call of Duty: Black Ops*, the next minute the police were hefting Jared to jail life; this week at a wedding, a month after the honeymoon, the groom's got cancer—terminal, only twenty-one years old.

These tragedies used to happen to some other people in distant places twice removed. Drugs, the busts and the overdoses, were reserved for screens and pages. Everyone in America seemed to have a diagnosis and a prescription. Everyone was in debt. And then cancer, of race, of politics, of offenses. And all these little kids at home in hospitals, suffering ailments with names as long as paragraphs. In the hell I just left, lives thrive beneath a dollar; here, one hundred dollars is a sentence, with hard labor.

There may be freedom in America but it is not for me. In Nigeria I could do anything, drive wherever; here, there are eyes on my shoulder ready to sue, to pull me over, there are offenses on every corner waiting to be incensed, illegalities known and ridiculous, triggers ready to be tripped, pulled with no warning. Should there be these many consequences to freedom? I miss Nigeria, the land of the free and lawless, where the police are your friend and you can hand them beers and bribes as you drive by with no papers. You might be disturbing the peace if you laugh too loud in America, you might be in trouble if you keep too straight a face. America is a tightrope, and even the best slip sometimes. Every day I feel like a boy again, in the presence of a heavy-handed parent with good intentions. How would I offend today? These are my chains in this land of the free.

I flew into America on the wings of literary promise. I was chasing literary heights that all the lights said were closer this way. But fantasy is a genre of fiction, and wands are hard to come by in any hell. I think now, daily, of what death said to the drowning girl: "You drown in three feet or in six, matters not to me."

But would they listen, those beer-clad young writers in Lagos's Freedom Park, when we tell them that where the grass is sparse means more could grow? Would they believe that *The New Yorker*, *The Paris Review*, *Best American Short Stories*, which we burn to have in Lagos, lie here in the library, issue after issue, year after year, unopened, unread? That the American writers we worship, we alone worship? Would they believe, those dear unschooled, unpublished, and uninitiated writers in Lagos, that their level of literary discourse and engagement is on par with grad and postgrad literature degree holders in America? They would not. I did not. What does it mean that I, yet alive, now speak the words of long-dead Dambudzo Marechera? "I was now actually on the soil where all these writers I had been studying had lived and died, and the reality was so disappointing."

In this new hell exist white denizens and black spirits, brown souls and unknown bodies, and trans and cis and more. All suffering from the other. These were not brands where I came from, but now here I am, suffering the consequences. Now that I am black, I have found that there are different shades of this hue, some to honor and others to dishonor.

To the well-adjusted whites in this hell, my accent means I am the other kind of black, the perhaps safe, exotic Mandingo warrior raised on a tree but good in bed and fluent in lioness. I am a closer breed to nature, can understand thunder and divine rain. I am the aww, and sometimes the cool. I am the vast arid plains, the grass. I am the Serengeti. They will cry for me and storm Twitter and the school senate on my behalf. All out of pity informed by the likes of CNN and encouraged by my kinsmen who come here spewing yarns of being former child soldiers, sex slaves, of being gay and hunted by an entire village. You cannot pour sand in the garri of your own kinsmen because their lies are almost true, if not to them, to some back in the motherland. But it hurts to be pitied and sorrowed over by people, some of whom are no better in health, wealth, and mind, on account of the single story.

In Nigeria, today, are many who believe that white people are constructed of missionary parts and can be trusted to be kindly and benevolent. And there are premises for their conclusions—J. D. O'Connell, my secondary school principal, was turbaned last week for "fifty years of meritorious service as principal." In all that time, since 1967, O'Connell must have left Minna four or five times to visit his country, Ireland. Black missionaries saving white worlds are not well known.

Every African visitor or immigrant knows of that white family who would seek your adoption and treat you like their own. This magnanimity they also extend to stray dogs and cats and iguanas. But an African with tales of woe stands a better chance of getting a room in the basement.

There are no reasons left to be a proud Nigerian, but still it is hard to suffer the indignity of pity. Especially as an artist. Art revels in its appreciation and acknowledgment, but there's nothing so diminishing as validation tainted or expressed from a place of pity. The gushing emails from some of your professors, shocked and awed by the quality of your output, soon begin to grate because you suspect you are being viewed through the lens of pity, appraised with considerations as an "other." There is such a thing as excellence despite being African. It is not a good thing. To the usual uncertainty and self-doubt of most creatives comes this new one: Are you a good writer because you are, or are you a good writer for an African? These depressives turn malignant in America.

In the American hell are many burdens new and unique to the fresh Nigerian. As a Nigerian in a place like Utah, I am the voice of the underworld. My opinion must be heard in every class, sought in every discourse, because ideas from the underworld are necessary for robust thoughts, for balance, for the edification of the white mind. It is very easy to succumb under the weight and tell people what they want to hear.

This is where I confess that I, too, have disgraced the ancestors by telling some unpalatable truths of Nigeria and Africa. For this, I die daily, reviving somewhat only to enjoy the shock and trauma that these African tales extract from my white listeners. I have told about the fourteen-year jail term for homosexuality in Nigeria. I have retold the testimony of Julius who claimed to have been a child soldier in a Nigerian city with no war. These tales move America.

The legend is that one of every four black people on earth is a Nigerian. The ship of the black race, therefore, cannot sail, the flag of black pride cannot fly without Nigeria. Hundreds of blacks returned to their roots, to Africa, to Nigeria during the black pride movement of the '70s. They could not stay. The ship was sinking with Nigeria at the helm. "I am not happy with Nigeria," said Nelson Mandela, "black people of the world need Nigeria to be great as a source of pride and confidence." This sentiment is still shared in the black world, especially these days when no good news is Nigerian. I am burdened then, with the guilt of much that is wrong with the black race.

In conversations with African American friends I try to defend, to explain Nigeria away, to argue that no, we are not a scourge to black pride. I sound sillier each time. And each night after these conversations, after another display of shame from my home country, I weep for the race, I mourn for the era when the black pride would be more of fact than blind faith. I know my country is an idiot, but I do not know what excuse other black nations have. Were I an African American, I too would be resentful of the African nations.

I have yet to learn the dangers of the American inferno. How do I learn to feel black? How do I not treat Black Lives Matter like All Lives Matter? When the American blacks rage about their black experience, do I have any right to speak? How do I remember to react when a white person uses the n-word in my presence? When is a white person just doing their job, or having a bad day, or just being drunk and not being racist? When are whites just being kind? How do I know that my failures and denials have nothing to do with my skin color? Would I need pills to shoulder the knowledge of these answers? The other blacks, the African Americans who have been here longer, they know the rules and see the threats coming. They have extra oil in their lamps. I am not angry enough to fight this war I just woke up in; I may yet embrace the enemy as a friend.

So I am sitting on a long thing—on the colored fence dividing America—buffeted upright by the shots from both sides, and I cannot fall to any side.

This was not the dream.

Oh, that life would be lighter. My nights would be shorter and my mornings would come adorned with joy. I long for the recent old days when there was no excuse to wake up and no reason to fret about it. Bring back the days when suicide was inconceivable and as distant from thoughts as the instances of its occurrence. But I see now that I am still harpooned by the curse of hope. And I do not want its pain.

This is where we've come, the legion that escaped one hell for another. This is where I've come, to the America of lights and dreams. And if I am better off I cannot tell.

ARAB PAST, AMERICAN PRESENT

Lauren Alwan

In the years my grandparents lived in their rambling, Spanish-style house in Southern California, they kept a Koran and a prayer rug in their bedroom hidden behind an ornate armchair. The chair, from Damascus, stood in one corner, grandly unused, its cushions upholstered in silk and the walnut frame set with mother-of-pearl. I never saw my grandparents use the Koran or the prayer rug. By the time I was born, they had fallen away from their practice of Islam.

My grandparents were Sunni, but after decades in the United States they'd become secular Muslims, with an identity lodged in the language, culture, attitudes, and customs they brought when they immigrated. After Islam, what remained was this: the Arabic spoken among my grandparents and their four sons; the meals we ate; the house with its Persian rugs and heavy Moorish Revival furniture; the letters scattered across bureaus and side tables, pages sent from Damascus and Beirut with their lines of Arabic script, and photographs of relatives I never met, at the beach, in a garden, or at home posed around a damask chair not unlike the ones in my grandparents' house.

My paternal grandfather, Muneer Alwan, first came to Brooklyn from Syria in 1911, and with his younger brothers, Faris, Saide, Fouad, and Mahmoud, launched a successful Atlantic Avenue bakery. Alwan Bros. Syrian Pastry quickly made a name for itself as a purveyor of confections, and for decades garnered regular coverage in the local press. In the square pink boxes shipped across the United States, and to Cairo, London, and Paris, there was baklava, pistachio bird's nests, Turkish delight. In summer, the shop sold exceptional ice cream made from pistachio, melon, or rose petals.

In the summer of 1921, my grandfather went back to Damascus to marry, and that fall, returned to New York with my grandmother, Fausya Zemberekçi, a new bride with waist-length chestnut hair and a Circassian complexion—fair and gray-eyed. She'd come from what was then Constantinople, fifteen years old, and on the subsequent honeymoon in Paris, impulsively had her hair chopped into a Western bob. At the time, she spoke only Turkish and the French she'd been tutored in at home. My grandfather taught her his dialect of Levantine Arabic and enrolled her in English classes at a Brooklyn adult school. They had four sons, the eldest my father, and raised their family in the close-knit community of Arab émigrés in Brooklyn.

Occasionally my father and his brothers talked about the

shop and the days in Brooklyn. The bakery was the center of their family life, a place the boys went after school or on weekends, and where each eventually learned some aspect of the business—baking bread, making pastry, the exacting methods of candy-making. Behind the shop in the bakery's kitchen, there was a table used expressly for rolling out pastry dough by means of a wooden dowel whose length matched the width of the work surface. In the light cast from an overhead window, my grandfather worked the dough to a legendary thinness, rolled until it draped over the table's edges like a bolt of cloth.

At its peak, the business was run by all five Alwan brothers. My grandmother never worked there, but she did stop in each day for spending money on the way to Fulton Street. If my grandfather hesitated to open the register for her, the story went, his brothers persuaded him otherwise. Dressed in a hat and a Persian lamb coat, she'd lunch at the counter in Abraham & Straus, content to people-watch and be admired for her clothes and jewelry. Shopping was her escape, a pursuit that countered homesickness, disappointment, and the unrelenting boisterousness of having four sons.

Years later, in California, my grandmother forgot her native Turkish, but she always remembered the days in Brooklyn. And when she reminisced, it wasn't about the Beyoglu district in the Constantinople of her youth, but of Fulton Street—its shops and clamoring streets that were so unlike the quiet, unpeopled sidewalks in her adopted corner of Los Angeles.

With each leg of my grandparents' journey—from Damascus and Istanbul to New York and finally Los Angeles—the markers of their previous lives fell away: my grandmother's first language, the Koran, the prayer rug, the community of Arab émigrés in Brooklyn. Though certain customs remained: Neither of my grandparents ever learned to drive, and they always spoke Arabic at home. They preferred my grandfather's Syrian cooking to what they called American food, and didn't cotton to eating in restaurants or taking vacations. In Los Angeles, they were content to live apart from the mainstream, within the bounds of home, family, and the community of Armenian and Lebanese immigrants who, like my grandparents, found California's weather and geography agreeably familiar.

In the assimilation that took place between the first and second generations, the tensions between the old and new were constant. When my father came of age, he didn't care to be matched with the young women my grandmother called Syrian girls. His brothers felt the same, and the result was four intercultural marriages, each a hybrid but uniform in its shedding of Arab identity and customs. None of the grandchildren in the third generation were taught to speak Arabic. Nothing of the religious or cultural identity was passed down. This, more than anything, brought about the break with our history: the missing knowledge of our ethnocultural past. Without it, there was only the sense of our difference, one that was at once deeply rooted and unfamiliar.

•

The term "Arab American" was coined in the 1960s as a rejection of the racial classification of "White," the only category available to people like my relatives on naturalization and census forms. According to *Arabs in America*, a historical resource of the University of North Carolina at Chapel Hill, the racial classification for Arab Americans has long been ambiguous, the legacy of a past in which immigrants from Greater Syria, the Arab province of the Ottoman Empire, were initially classified as Turks, and so grouped with Asians under the category of "Oriental." For this early wave of Arab immigrants, the misclassification was not only inaccurate, but linked them with the anti-Asian immigration laws in effect at that time.

After the First World War, immigrants arriving from the newly partitioned countries of Syria, Lebanon, Jordan, and later, Palestine, chose White over Asian on their immigration papers. Identifying as white was a way to thwart the bias of anti-immigrant sentiment that had expanded to many Middle Eastern countries. In 1911, when my grandfather first immigrated, and in 1921, when my grandmother arrived at Ellis Island, the classification of White might have been seen as a necessity for being successful in the United States. The classification enabled citizenship, but also acceptance and inclusion. It may also have enabled them to buy the family home in Los Angeles.

In 1949, the year before he retired, my grandfather took a train to California, where he'd heard from friends that Los Angeles, with its fruit trees, flowers, and backdrop of mountains, was "just like Damascus." A Lebanese friend in real estate had a listing, a house with a private garden, Palladian windows, and plenty of room for the family. At the time, the Federal Housing Authority's discriminatory laws were still in force, and the Spanish-style house my grandfather immediately loved would not have been exempt. Contemporary maps of the redlined districts show the house was located in an A zone, or what the FHA designated as an uppermost grade of *housing level security*, where non-whites were denied homeownership through discriminatory lending practices. Having lived for decades in an established immigrant community in Brooklyn, my grandparents likely didn't encounter bias or a great deal of anti-Arab sentiment, but in Los Angeles, my grandfather, a businessman who kept up with civic affairs, may have known that being seen as non-white could be an obstacle to home ownership.

Suppressing certain traits and customs enabled first-generation immigrants like my grandparents to assimilate, and when necessary, gain acceptance in white circles. My grandfather, with his imposing stature, tweed suits, and sun-browned scalp, projected authority and business acumen, while my grandmother, with her careful grooming and gold jewelry and French air, conveyed a certain urbanity. These traits may well have aided them when they moved to Los Angeles, but they always preferred the like-minded community of immi-grants they found there. These were similarly business-driven first-generation families, merchants and manufacturers who held on to certain customs. Like my grandparents, they enter-tained in formal living rooms with tea and cake, and as guests, always dressed for the occasion and were sure to arrive with a sack in hand of fruit picked that morning.

Our family spent more than five decades in the house in Los Angeles, a life built around the rhythms of cooking, housekeeping, and gardening. Mornings, my grandfather would dress as he had in Brooklyn—starched white shirt, flan-nel trousers, wing tips, cardigan sweater—and make his way down the winding driveway to retrieve the *Los Angeles Times* for the daily stock reports. Mornings were for baking and cooking the evening meal, which was always done by lunch in order to spend the afternoon in the garden. As a child, I was terrifically bored on those afternoons, when little occurred but contemplating the garden along with snippets of conversation and occasional fruit eating. Years later, an apricot tree sprouted in the backyard, the result of my grandmother eating apricots and tossing the pits into the flower bed.

The house and its garden was all my grandparents seemed to need. Even when their sons left home and the days were gone when my uncles and their friends emptied my grandfa-ther's pantry, consuming elliptical loaves of bread and fat braids of fresh cheese, the pattern of life in the rambling house was the same.

•

In the years I spent with my grandparents, no one ever said the word *Arab*. It didn't matter that the furniture was Moorish Revival, or that the floors were laid with Persian rugs, or that the only picture on the wall in the living room was a sepia plate of my grandfather (framed by embroidery work of flowers and leaves and stitched by my grandmother on the occasion of their engagement).

Whatever we were—and certainly we were different—each time I stepped foot into the cloistered, carpeted, impermeable bastion my grandparents built, the puzzle of the unspoken world and my own culturally mixed place within it presented itself anew. Each year, I felt the difference more sharply—though it was not the kind of sharpness that made details more clear, but the kind that exists at arm's length, at once engrained and unexplained.

I think of my mother's parents, Jewish New Yorkers whose ancestors were swept by the diaspora from Russia to the Pale of Settlement, west to Eastern Europe and New York's Lower East Side. In my maternal grandparents' house, the word *Jewish* was constantly spoken. There was no question we were Jews, and my mixed heritage never prevented my Jewish grandfather from encouraging my sister and me to identify as Jewish. He urged us to study Judaism, to go to Israel, live on a kibbutz, marry a Jewish boy. Our mother was Jewish, after all, so Jewishness was our right in regard to its culture—our food, our thinking, ourselves.

As affirming as that was, my bicultural experience was one of divisions and cultural tensions, the result of my parents' mixed marriage that ultimately couldn't surmount the obstacles. Thinking of those differences now, I understand better how meaningful it is for a young person to hear one's identity spoken aloud, and yet for me, that never quite helped. As positive as my Jewish heritage is, it's my Arab identity that pulls at me, as though the invisibility is an unfinished narrative with missing chapters and details that keep the story from being fully known.

•

In the week after the 2016 presidential election, the FBI released a report on hate crime statistics in the United States that showed incidents of harassment, intimidation, and assault on Muslims increased by 67 percent between 2014 and 2015. According to the Southern Poverty Law Center, the number exceeds that of 2001, the year when attacks on the United States by Al Qaeda resulted in 481 hate crimes, the highest recorded. The surge took place during the run-up to the primaries and there was another surge after Election Day. The Southern Poverty Law Center also reported that by November 11, more than two hundred incidents of intimidation and harassment were committed. These included confrontations, vandalism, and epithets directed at individuals, many of which included references to the Trump campaign. The most frequent incidents reported were characterized as anti–African American, anti-immigrant, and anti-Muslim.

For years there was silence around my family's larger story, an absence of facts and details that might have illuminated the thoughts and feelings my grandparents had about their Arab past and American present. Though it's also true that as a teenager, I found not knowing a kind of relief. As a family outsider who couldn't speak Arabic and had only the vaguest sense of history, not knowing exempted me from having to explain a confusing and foreign-seeming part of my heritage to others. Now, as the nationalist rhetoric against Muslim and Arab immigrants increases, I have a different view on the invisibility that was passed to me by my grandparents.

After the 2016 election, the family history of invisibility takes on new meaning as people with our same ethnic, religious, and cultural heritage are targeted based on their affiliations. To date, the rhetoric around Muslim registration centers on immigrants from countries termed high-risk. Yet this targeting, which blurs the distinction between enemy and ethnic identity, has troubling historical parallels to Executive Order 9066, when racial targeting during the Second World War led to authorized forced relocation of Japanese Americans to incarceration camps—families consisting of both the immigrant generation and the second American-born generation. Invisibility feels impossible now, when the president has promised to ban Muslim immigration and talks of reinstating the post-9/11 registry of Muslims. It's impossible when the president has promised to search out people in their communities, to ensure they'll be "signed up in different places," a euphemism for a registration system that will discriminate on the basis of nationality and religion.

When I think of the family legacy that included silence as a way to belong, I see it against those individuals targeted for registration despite their legal entitlement to protection by the Constitution. Today, I wonder if my Arab surname, even two generations out, could be seen as an identifiable threat.

Even though my grandparents chose not to pass along traits of Arab identity, as my grandmother aged, in her encroaching dementia the past became more vivid and crucial to her and she disclosed events and feelings that had previously gone unspoken. She described the dismay she had as a girl at the news of her arranged marriage, and the disappointment in middle age of moving to Los Angeles—to the house she'd always wanted, but adjacent to the mountains on a quiet residential street—the isolation made her long for Brooklyn. Her story as I gleaned it was one of a repeated breach between the known and unknown worlds, a separation from people and things she knew that cycled over the course of her life. A conflict of near and far, known and unknown, remembered and forgotten.

Part of that separation, I see now, is her view of me not as Arab, but American. To my grandmother, I was what she called an American girl—my first language is English, and being born in the States, I have an independence my foremothers never knew. Along with that, I have another privilege: I was born at a time that made me witness to two distinct eras. I was a bridge between the world my grandparents came from and the one they gave to their descendants. I know something of how it was for my grandparents Muneer and Fausya Alwan to live a cloistered and perhaps intentionally invisible life. For new Muslim and Arab immigrants to the United States, that privilege of invisibility is a thing of the past and may never return.

•

In 2004, my grandmother died at age ninety-eight, and the house in Los Angeles was sold. When the rooms were cleared out, the Koran and prayer rug went to one of my uncles. I have one of the upholstered chairs, though its silk had gone tattered long before, and the mother-of-pearl marquetry turned brittle and chipped. The house had been in the family more than fifty years, but the life there had vanished long before the sale, the result of scattered relations and bonds that didn't hold. Yet vestiges remain in the third generation—in our names, in our features and assorted shades of olive skin, and in a family history that grows dimmer by the year.

Who's to say—had the family heritage been passed on differently, the ties might be stronger now. But when I think of my Arab identity, I see it as through a glass, a world without explanation, where the viewer is left to draw conclusions based not on what she is told, but only on those things she can see. If my grandparents and others in that first generation of immigrants had chosen to pass along those traits and markers of identity, their culture might be better understood in this political moment. Maybe, now, the naming and sharing of our history can help bring about a better understanding of who we truly are, and exactly what is behind the designation of Arab in America.

How to Write About Your Ancestral Village

Steph Wong Ken

First, you have a nervous breakdown. Your chest tightens and you stop breathing over the keyboard in your office to let the voices chiming "Who are you" and "What are you" occupy the air in your brain. You think about the time it takes to explain at parties that you are mixed—from China *and* Jamaica, yes really—though you'll always be just exotic enough to men who want to date you. You think about the man in the white van who yelled at you this morning on the street: "Better go back to China, bitch." Initially, you thought, fuck you. And now, hyperventilating at your desk, you think, why not? You buy a one-way ticket to Beijing, tell your mother you are traveling for two months alone across the country to figure out if China might be the answer: a place where you can find a part of yourself, or maybe half, down at the bottom of a deep red hole.

"At least look up your cousin Kris," your mother tells you after she is done arguing, done telling you this is just another one of your foolish notions.

Kris, your only surviving blood relative in China, lives and works in Shenzhen, the Overnight City of progress on the edge of the South China Sea. You pass out on the plane and wake up in the future, work your way down the country, down to him, from hostel to homestay, Great Wall to industrial city, monument to noodle house to factory town. You accept your role as listener, observer, amateur photographer, taking hundreds of photographs of the imperial seal stamped into green-gray marble, the knotted limbs of bonsai trees, the mah-jongg games in the public squares, the man drawing Chinese characters on a stone slab in the park. You move through a sea of Chinese faces day after day until you blend enough to startle a Dutch family at a teahouse, who stare at you, slack-jawed, when real American English falls out of your mouth.

You are exhausted by the time you get to Shenzhen. Waiting at the train station, your backpack is too much weight to manage but you got yourself into this quest so you bend over like the Chinese women in the market, twisted down like boughs.

Your cousin appears, the same with flecks of gray in his hair, and you embrace awkwardly, almost like family. He puts you up in a chain hotel at the back of a foot massage parlor, close to his apartment building down the street.

"My place is too small for the both of us," he says.

The chain hotel is filthy and depressing. The woman at the

front desk doesn't speak English and doesn't smile. She must think you are your cousin's mistress or a mute who only owns one pair of shoes.

Before China, you hadn't seen your cousin in over a decade. Throughout your childhood, he would appear periodically at your aunt's house in Miami, home from university on summer break. In dress-up clothes and Auntie's heels, you would stumble into him upstairs in his old room, reading Mandarin language books and practicing his Chinese calligraphy on pads of white paper. Once, he asked you if you wanted to learn how to write your family name. He placed you on the chair by his desk and put the brown bamboo brush between your fingers, dripping with charcoal ink. Wrapping his fingers over yours, you drew a long vertical line together, followed by three descending horizontal lines, lifting the brush lightly with each stroke.

"Our name means 'King,'" he told you as the ink dried. He ripped the paper off the pad and gave it to you, the first and only Chinese character you would learn to draw.

You shed your backpack on the stained hotel bedspread and meet your cousin on the noisy street corner for dinner. He takes you to a Hong Kong–style dinner with pink plastic cups and you ask about his trip ten years ago to his ancestral village with his father, your uncle by marriage, Uncle T. In a rickety rental car, they drove for four hours, changing one flat tire on a road meant for bicycles and cattle. After walking through sleepy farmland and communal gardens, father and son discovered the graveyard, lit firecrackers over the headstones marked *Chin*. The fizzle and smoke dance is a call to the dead, a forget-me-not for you and yours in the next life. A warding off for the family name, just in case.

But you do not belong to the plots of Chin. Your Chinese comes from your mother's side, the Lyns, who lived poor in stone homes somewhere in the belly of the south. Grandmother Dorothy was of the Hakka people, a nomadic tribe who lived in round stone structures, fortified from the outside world. When she married Grandfather, she became Fook Tai, and left China on a boat to join him in Jamaica, to start a life better than *poor*. Because records are missing and your mother is not forthcoming, you don't know the exact coordinates of your grandmother's village, the home Fook Tai left behind.

Still, you tell your cousin, over steamed duck and rice, you are ready to visit the ancestors, any ancestors. You almost say you would like to go *back* to the village, as if you've been there, breathed the air, licked the soil, once before. You're not sure where this habit comes from, this tendency to talk through ghosts. He tells you he'll take you to the Chin one, if he can still remember the way. Then, after a pause, he says, "I guess it doesn't matter, really, which one you go to."

•

On the train to the village, you feel an itch crawling up your back, under your shirt, sweat soaking into your bra, and though you really want to, you do not release the rubber strap attached to the slick ceiling of the train.

"Back then, there were no trains, no towers, none of this," Kris says as you struggle to stay upright.

"How did you feel when you got there?" you ask him over the metallic hum of the tracks. Your cousin puts out one bony finger, leans over to answer a call. He speaks away from you in Mandarin, not that you could understand him anyway. He has been doing this a lot during your visit: secretive phone calls, vague answers about where he lives or what he does for work, brushing off your inquires into his friends or his job in the infamous Overnight City.

You turn to the window and face the impossible skyscrapers, buoyed by smog, like someone running their hand through a palette of chemical grays. Arms and legs hang down from the concrete balconies. Children gape at the passing train car, tangled up in clothesline. The grandmas chat in the narrow seats beside you, laughing over their padded shoes and stuffed metal carts. A man curls his head toward his chest, cell phone pressed over his heart while he dozes standing up. When the wheels grind to a stop and the doors fly open, the car fills with soggy air, the stink of coal. When you thought of China, you never imagined the dust or the smells. You pictured the red hole that might help you make sense of your body, your blood, your face.

As the train pulls into the stop for the village, you try on your Fook Tai look, from the grandmother your mother says you resemble when you are stunned or asleep. If your cousin notices, he doesn't react.

"Wo men zou ba," he says over his shoulder as he moves

through the crowd, his voice clipped at the end of one of the ten phrases you can recognize in Mandarin. You stick your head out into a sea of people bumping against one another like ghosts in the haze. This is what you came for, isn't it? You push past the grandmas, the stiff body of the man sleeping, and follow.

You find out the name of your grandmother's village in an email from your mother, *Tai Shui Ten village,* but by the time you read it, you have left Shenzhen, your cousin, and that part of China, your fifty-pound backpack a little lighter on your back. Still, like good-luck charms, you keep the smog masks, the hand sanitizer, the four-pack of tissues given to you by your mother in a pouch.

"Don't eat the street food," she warned before you left. "Don't touch the door handles."

Your mother has never been to China, has only heard stories of her mother's sad, nineteenth-century life, but she maintains a picture of the country created by television, newspapers, and Pearl S. Buck. The night before your departure, she gave you a small Canadian flag to attach to the front of your backpack.

"Don't forget where you come from," she said as she pressed the metal into your hands. A double statement maybe, or her way of telling you this trip is a mistake.

In the bright green cab, your cousin eyes the driver's laminated photo ID, says, "What's up," in a tell-me-more tone. The driver responds in grunts and haws, his fingers light on the steering wheel as the cab careens across the winding road. The road has the jet-black seal of new asphalt. You tune out the conversation as it shifts into language beyond the basics and count ten construction cranes in the valley, their white latticed arms all jutting out in the same direction. Forward, you think as the cab passes half-completed housing developments, road-side restaurants with empty tables and chairs. The cabdriver is talking faster, one hand slicing the air, gesturing out the window. You race through the flat, gray landscape at incredible speed.

"He says this is all new," your cousin translates. "He says, now it's all part of modern China."

Your cousin and the driver keep talking. Your mind wanders to a recent email from your mother. *How's Kris?* Your mother wrote, *Are you getting along?* Emailing your mother began as an excuse to use the free hostel computers, a way to stave off the loneliness of eating solo on the side of a city road. You tell yourself you are creating a digital travel journal for the future you, to confirm later that you did in fact see the Forbidden City and ten hundred statues of Mao. But really, you are writing the emails to remind your mother that your trip has an essential purpose, beyond a backpacker's holiday. Every time you report the details of your meal with Chinese locals at a noodle house, you are discovering some hidden part of your identity, the parts she is too busy or ashamed to examine. Every monument you stare at, built by Chinese hands, brings you closer to a fuller sense of self.

Out the window of the cab, you glimpse a slice of lush green, thatched houses by a row of fields, like a grimy version of a Chinese silkscreen. *There*, you think as the cab rolls on, toward the stone archway, the town square. When you get out, you thank the driver quickly with your foreign accent. Your cousin is on his phone again, his back to you in the crowded street. You lean over and hand the driver the tattered red bills, fifty yuan for the fare.

At the center of the archway a stone plaque says NIHU in Chinese characters, and behind it, a printed sign says HUANG'S PLASTIC AND METALS. Your cousin marvels at the hair salons, pool halls, herbal medicine shops.

"The driver wasn't joking about progress," he says, and you remember he is seeing this all for the first time too. All that farmland, all the communal gardens of ten years ago buried under factories and towers for the workers, the nonlocals. You see the beginnings of a skyline in the town, a megacity in the making. This is what your ancestral village probably looks like, too.

•

The town square is empty save for garbage and stray dogs licking their paws by a flowering tree. Women read under hair dryers, and an electronics store shows a movie on a stack of televisions that features Chow Yun-Fat, a famous Chinese star and Hakka, like half of you. On screen, he is the villain with the crew cut, holding a knife to a man's throat. While your cousin looks for someone on the street who can identify as local or talk about the past, you end up in front of a narrow stone home, Tulou style, overrun by choking vines and flat-leaf weeds. You run your hand over a hunk of glass, one in a row sticking out of the low fence, held in place by cement. Meant to keep out birds, but you can't help thinking the glass is meant to cut you or anyone else who tries to set foot in this abandoned place. Your cousin is talking loudly with a slim man in a navy uniform standing by the road and then he calls you over, says, "Hey, he knows about Jamaica." The security guard has a creased brown face and sun-spotted hands. His family emigrated to Jamaica in the 1890s and never returned.

"No one visits," the man says, stretching his tanned fingers toward the empty street.

"Well, except for us." Your cousin translates your words and the man smirks into the dust.

"Yes," the old guard says, "only you have returned."

Whenever you waxed poetic about visiting the ancestral village, your mother would casually mention your friend Paul. "Remember his enlightening experience?" she would demand, leaning on the story like a tale of folly and woe. The arduous journey of Paul, your half-white, half-Chinese friend, mixed up and a little fucked up like you, who tried to go *back*. Took the train ride, the car ride, and walked thirty minutes by foot until he found the sacred place his aunt-who-knows-all mentioned once before her death. Knocked on the door and readied his camera for photos with the son of the father of his father, still living in the village and maintaining the same livelihood on the land. The man finally undid the latch, opened the door. Paul, flexing his best Mandarin, said, "Hello. I have your name. We're family." The man looked him over, this light-skinned, mixed-up kid at his doorstep, and let out a laugh right in the kid's face.

Thought I was just another laowai, Paul tells you and your mother later. *A foreigner*, pulling one of those harmless jokes foreigners can't help but play.

The security guard has a firm grip when you shake his hand goodbye. You hold it briefly like a hot stone before falling behind your cousin's salt-and-pepper hair. The sun slides past the lip of the archway and then you are both somehow in the middle of the town's night market, tables and tables of cheap children's toys and clothing, fresh fruit, and bugs barbecued on sticks. Your cousin tries talking to one of the older women selling taro root under a blue tarp, and you catch the eye of the snake-oil man, a bulbous figure standing behind vials of brown liquid and a glistening, preserved snake. He cups the withered snake head and tries to sell in four tones, chatter that lulls you now like background music. Relieved, you rely on your standard nod and faint smile, your if-I-shut-my-mouth-I-am-one-of-you move. *That's right, Fook Tai*, you think as the putrid brown oil is thrust into your face, *I never knew you*. The woman talking to your cousin by the blue tarp suddenly turns aggressive, his questions getting in the way of her sales, and you untangle yourself from the dead snake head as she flicks her birdlike hands toward your cousin's chest, the international sign for "get out of my space."

Face flushed, your cousin sets his mouth tight against his collar, pulls out his phone. You feel an ache growing in the pit of your stomach and remember you both haven't eaten in hours. You pay the vendor ten yuan for two paper bags of peanuts, hold one out to your cousin.

"Now what?" you say to him. He bites down, cracks open a shell.

"Not sure," he says. "The woman mentioned something down the road, something we might want to see."

At the end of a long trail of peanut shells, you and your cousin stand in front of the stunning structure. MISSION HILL, the blazing ten-foot sign reads beside columns of trees, and then in smaller script, *China's Largest Luxury Golf Course.* Back in the night market, under a blue tarp, the taro root seller is laughing her head off. *One of those harmless jokes foreigners can't help but play.*

"Damn," your cousin manages as he chucks the empty paper bag into a bush. Picturing all those Chin plots, all those firecrackers, bulldozed for a killer par 3. You stand close to your cousin, watch him watch the luxury sign flash bright in the night air. You know there is no section in the unofficial guide to the ancestral village that explains this kind of degradation. On the walk back to town, your cousin strides with his head bent, eager to get out of this place, back to the familiar rules of the Overnight City. Treading behind him under the trees, you recall the cab ride, that brief, sweet slice of pure green out the window. *There*, you think, finally remembering.

You find it in the pitch dark, by its marshy smell. The fields appear thick and ripe even in the dim glare of the only light on the road, the fire from an iron stove. Behind the stove, shanties made of tin and wood line the dirt path, maybe five, maybe ten. As a sign of welcome, a man rips by you on a motorbike, trailing exhaust over the pathway. Your cousin moves toward an open doorway, a man watching television and eating from a bowl. You take out your camera and set the zoom on the fields, the shanties, the path, but the photographs will come out blurry and dark, not worth showing your mother later. The kids have started to gather around you and your cousin, in your travel clothes, your running shoes, the camera dangling in your hand. You bend down to show one child the photographs you have taken: the land, the shanties, the kids in track pants and plastic slippers. A woman appears by a doorway and shoos the children inside. She slides off a pair of rubber boots and deposits them by the threshold, gently shuts the door behind her. Your mother's words vibrate in your ears. *Fook Tai left by boat. She never wanted to go back. Why should you?*

You find your cousin in front of a shanty, in conversation with a man with no shirt and no shoes.

"They're not local either," your cousin says, "they rent the land from the Hakka."

"And where are the Hakka?" you ask the man, though you already know his answer. The man's face is impassive and unforgettable.

"They live in big houses," the man says, his words flowing through your cousin to you. "Somewhere far away from here."

CAREFREE WHITE GIRLS, CAREFUL BROWN GIRLS

Cinelle Barnes

If I were a white girl, I'd want to be the kind that's just like you, K.L.

You used to roll out of bed just before noon, after a night at Surf Bar and Sand Dollar Social Club, and mount your longboard onto the jeep, drive to the Washout, and ride Carolina's biggest waves until the northeast groundswell rested. Then you were off to work: to deliver drugs. You picked up packages from some beach shack or surf shop, or met a frat boy at the dunes on Folly. Same beach where the best female surfers from the East Coast and Puerto Rico gather every year in June: the Folly Beach Wahine Classic, the first surf competition in the country to cater only to women and girls. Wahine: Hawaiian for "woman."

But it was on another Charleston beach, another stretch of dunes, that we met. You were at Isle of Palms to teach surf lessons; I was there to learn, to redevelop my core strength after giving birth, to do something I'd always wanted to do, to do it now before it was too late—before motherhood took over every part of me, before I surrendered my dreams for life with a family.

"I'm a mom, too," you said. "I'm K.L." You knew my anxious energy, you pulled me into yours. We became friends right there, right before the roaring ocean, a blond chick and a Filipina, because I had a whimpering baby on my hip and you had a whining preteen at your side, and we both knew we weren't spending our day at the beach with men today. Today was Wahine Time.

"You're one of the teachers?" I said, exhaling the salt air I had gulped in, relieved that I didn't have to lie on some man's board and receive instructions from him, relieved that I didn't have to slide in and out of the water in a swimsuit with a man watching my every move, relieved that this first time wouldn't be a trigger, that it wouldn't remind me of every time I've lain next to or under a man, confused, unwilling, with the body of a resting cat but the face of a petrified dog. "Where do I sign?"

You handed me a clipboard of waivers and told me who you and your group were. "We're Christian surfers who give free surf lessons—I guess you can say that many of us were saved by surfing."

This was the rehearsed part of your speech, the only line from you that I thought came from somewhere other than your natural edge, your cool, that part of you that I saw in me—that small but strong propensity for risk, for chance, for the surf I was eager to meet. You held my baby while I practiced my paddle on the sand, and as your daughter taught my nephew, who was spending the summer with us, how to pop up on a board. You took me out to the water, told me to paddle harder, to wait, to go catch that wave.

I fell off the board many times, sometimes swallowing water or inhaling it, but you yelled, waist-deep in the water and holding my baby, "Get back on the board! Do it again!" I couldn't quit because I knew you wouldn't let me. I knew that you knew how to be hard on me, that you knew what a little push could make me do, how a little try could turn into a dare, a dare into an obsession, an obsession into an addiction. You knew this latent part of me, and you played it well.

It was sundown soon after my first successful try at getting my feet on the board and it was time for each of us to head home and make dinner, to do the dishes and laundry, to be mom again, to think of the waves as we fell asleep. I closed my eyes thinking of what a good day it was, how accomplished I felt, how much I liked you.

I emailed you the next morning, asked if you would like to come over for tea, and you responded within an hour. When my phone buzzed, I sprang onto the couch to reach for my phone. I had never been this excited for a playdate or a mom date because I had never met a white or Southern mom that I identified with as much as I did with you.

You came the following week, and between the email and your knock on the door, I thought of all that I wanted to tell you, how I would get you to tell me your truth. Did our proclivity for dangerous sports (before surfing, I snowboarded, rappelled, open-water jet-skied, snorkeled with orcas, bungee-jumped, and played soccer so fiercely, I once headed a ball so hard that I almost went blind in my right eye) not mean that we each had a past?

You sat down in front of the cup of tea I had made for you, never drank it, and instead sipped the protein smoothie you had brought with you. "I'm trying to be healthy," you said. "Health*ier.* Tryin' to take care of my body after years of neglecting it."

I watched you let the tea cool, your fingers teetering on the edge of the table then twirling and fidgeting with a tuft of your sun-bleached hair. You weren't like this at all in the water. I started to think that this was wrong—maybe I didn't really want to be your friend. I tried to think of something to say to ease us both, but you finally said, "Just ask what you want to ask."

I had interviewed many people before you, in journalism school and for my first newspaper job in Georgia. But here I was, taking a moment before asking, "Who were you before you were a surf instructor?"

You smiled at me then looked away, out the window, your blue eyes shimmering in the light like the ocean. You opened your mouth but paused. I thought that you were trying to decide whether to give me the truth or your rehearsed lines, so I said, "I'll tell you mine after."

You smiled again, but kept your eyes off me, and didn't look at me until you finished your story. You began, "I was a drug delivery girl. I transported coke from the city to the beach, and back, and sometimes to anywhere between here and New York." During our surf lesson, I had told you that I moved from New York, so I knew you were telling me this last detail to circle it back to me—to make sure I'd tell you *my* story.

"Was it always cocaine?" I said.

"Coke, Ecstasy, Xanax . . . whatever they pressed in their home labs, whatever they put in my beach bag, whatever I could hide in my bikini bottoms or boardshorts."

"How'd you get into it?"

You told me that you were just a local surfer girl, a Betty, a cute blonde who didn't want to go to college. You wanted to surf instead, to be like those locals who lived simply, had enough money for rent, food, and board wax; who waited tables at night and woke up to shred the gnar. It was going well until the beach and the city grew in popularity and the price of everything went up. You had tried coke just for the heck of it, because all the kids were doing it, but when an ex-boyfriend asked if you wanted to make money, you said yes. He hooked you up with a friend and the friend's boss, and the next time you mounted your board onto the jeep, you were loading a backpack of goods, too. They also gave you some to keep, to sniff. You drove into historic downtown and up and down the coast high, euphoric, but most important, immune to getting caught.

"It was a gig, a job, then a lifestyle."

Not once were you stopped or pulled over, you said. Not once did anyone suspect that you had something other than sunscreen in your waterproof sack. "Nobody will stop a young blond girl, that's the truth," you said. This was when I grew angry with you, when I wanted to scrap our week-old friendship.

"You're right," I said. "I've never transported drugs, never even done drugs, but I've been stopped and IDed at all sorts of places."

You finally looked away from the window and looked at me. "Your turn," you said.

"I was undocumented for eight years." Now I was the one looking away. "If you wanna know what that's like, just think the opposite of your story. I had to live as quietly as possible, be low-key at all times, even though I'd never committed a crime. I've never even shoplifted or vandalized, not even as a teen. I couldn't travel by plane or Amtrak, couldn't even order a margarita without making up a whole lie about forgetting my ID at home. If there was a checkpoint at a subway stop, I'd walk home. I was in perpetual hiding."

I told you of other instances when my identity was in question, when if I said the wrong thing or looked at the guard or the cop the wrong way, I could attract the wrong kind of attention, get IDed and interrogated, get sent to a detention center, or get deported. In college, when I applied for paid internships, despite my grades and writing knowledge, I got turned down semester after semester because I couldn't fill out a W-9. I accepted, instead, unpaid research or marketing positions or internships that didn't fulfill university credits.

When my then-boyfriend, now-husband proposed to me, and we had to acquire a marriage license from New York City Hall, the clerk whispered to the other clerk, showed her my forms, and said, "Just a minute." When they returned, they returned with a cop and the office director, asked my fiancé to wait outside and to hold my phone and purse, took me to a back room behind the copiers, and interrogated me. They asked me how I entered the country from the Philippines, and I said through adoption.

They asked me why I was adopted at sixteen, when I was old enough to drive, and I said that I'd been asking the same thing all my life—why did no one rescue me sooner? They asked me how I became undocumented after being adopted, and I said that their laws said I was too old to receive naturalization benefits, and that it took too long for our lawyer and the judge to file and stamp the hundreds of pages of required documents. They asked me why I didn't have an entry for "Father of the Bride" in the marriage license application, and I said that my adoptive parent was a widow. You don't need a man to give a minor a chance at life.

Finally, and I knew it was coming, they asked, "Young lady, how can we be sure that you're not marrying this man as a mail-order bride?"

"Oh, we're doing stereotypes now? I see!" I got up from the chair.

"Sit back down, young lady." I didn't sit back down and they didn't let me out, not until I proved that I wasn't purchased into the country. When I said that my fiancé was a graduate student with no money to buy a wife, that I had plans of attending grad school myself, the clerk finally took my application fee and stamped my form.

"Congrats," the clerk said without a smile as she handed over the marriage license.

Half a year after the interrogation in Manhattan, I found myself defending my identity again—this time in Atlanta. I needed antibiotics for a UTI and the most convenient place to get the prescription was the CVS MinuteClinic. The nurse practitioner on shift that day was a low-voiced woman who only looked up from her clipboard when you didn't answer quickly enough. After asking for my symptoms, and if I made the habit of peeing after sex, she asked, "That guy outside, is he really your husband?"

I showed her my ring.

"That don't mean a thing, hon."

"We've been married a few months. He was my boyfriend of four years."

"You sure he didn't pick you out of many at the airport?" She was referring to Atlanta's reputation as one of the busiest ports for sex trafficking and mail-order brides. I told her again that all I needed was an antibiotic, thanked her for looking out for me, and reached out my hand for the pills. She handed me the bottle and said, "You girls just always conning people or people are conning you, is all."

One Christmas, a cashier wouldn't sell me Earl Grey tea and a bag of pretzels because I did not look like the name on my credit card. "You don't look like a Barnes to me. This ain't yours." I asked her if she was looking for a Romero or a Gomez or a Lee, and all she said was, "We experience a lot of theft during the holidays, miss."

I told you these stories, K.L., and I waited for you to say something, maybe apologize for how easily you could get away with crime. But you said nothing. Instead, you got up and walked to the sink to empty your smoothie tumbler and rinse it, and you walked over to the freezer for ice like you'd walked to it many times, like you'd been in that kitchen to cook or eat or laugh or cry, like you owned the one place that was mine. I was furious at you now, or I was furious at the idea of you, of who you represented: white women everywhere who could, like you taught me how to slip on and off the board, fluidly slip in and out of spaces, toy with danger, give danger a name, call it a gig, a job, a lifestyle.

"You didn't drink your tea," I said.

You just shrugged, because you had that power, that privilege, too. In my culture, in Filipino culture, you don't turn down your host. You eat and drink what they serve you, you don't stop consuming until they stop bringing you things.

I started hoping for the baby to wake up from her nap so I could retrieve her from the crib and make it seem like it was time for you to leave. But the baby stayed asleep. *Must be the clouds*, I thought. A storm was rolling in, which meant the baby was falling into a deeper sleep, which also meant you'd avoid driving in the downpour and stay. I had to think of something that could make our time together bearable, but I didn't have to. You sat back down at the table with me, poured the now-room-temperature tea into your tumbler of ice, and took a sip.

"I'm not much of a hot tea kinda girl," you said and took a

sip again. "Baby's sleeping well, that's good. It's good to get a break."

"Yeah," I said, "motherhood's exhausting."

"It is, but having a daughter made me leave all that shit," you said, and this was when I started trusting you again, because what I hadn't told you was that before I was adopted and became undocumented, I was living in an abusive home. When I got out, I dealt with my previous trauma by self-injuring with needles and blades, and by starving myself. I also slept around, even dated one of my professors. Nothing criminal, nothing that would hurt anybody else—just myself. That all ended when I found out I was pregnant. Like you, I let all that shit go when I became aware of a human growing inside me, swimming in my uterus, paddling in to join me in the come-and-go, to rescue me from drowning.

I looked up and you were in tears. You were crying into the tea. I reached for your hand to rub it and to tell you I was okay now, that was all over. And you said, "I'm not crying because of that. I'm crying because I thought you didn't like me. I don't have a lot of mom friends, I don't fit in that world."

"Neither do I."

We hugged and you went home and we didn't see each other again except for a chance encounter at the beach. You had told me what it was like to be you, and I had told you what it was like to be me. We couldn't have traded places even if we wanted to. We were born into the skin we were in, destined for each of our circumstances. I can only guess that there was guilt on your part, an undertow of disdain on mine.

But still, I think of you, and I think of how I like you just fine, K.L. I even want to be you, live through you. I want you to keep surfing, to live dangerously, to be cool. I would like you even if you committed crime again, if you dared to go back to living so close to the edge. Why would it matter? You'd get away with it. Not me. I'm brown, an immigrant. I'm forever clean. But you'd get away with danger. For both of us. For those parts of you and me that are just underneath, that are brewing, coming to a swell, like rip current backwashing from the shore, pulling to the deep.

RETURN TO PARTITION

Nur Nasreen Ibrahim

When a seven-year-old girl made her way across India on a clattering, wheezing train in 1947, smoke rose from villages in the distance. Mustard and wheat fields, usually peppered with farmers tending to their crops, were empty. Long lines of bedraggled refugees were a common sight on the landscape, some moving west, to Pakistan, and others east, to India. Soldiers escorted some, others hitched rides on carts, trucks, anything they could find. Some were escaping the violence. Others were trudging toward violence. Partition was imminent.

The little girl, Nasreen, along with her mother and sister, had tried twice to catch a train out of India. On August 9, 1947, they reached the Delhi train station hoping to join the rest of their family who had already left for Pakistan. At the time, thousands of people, many of whom were Muslims trying to go to Pakistan, were jostling for spots on the trains, desperate to leave as news of unrest grew. The irritable, overwhelmed station manager in Delhi curtly informed them that since they had no reservations, they could not take this train.

A state away, Saeed was awaiting the British Army division. The future of the young Indian soldier was uncertain. Although he expected to leave and join his family in Pakistan, he had not received his orders yet. In October 1947, he would receive a form from his British superiors, asking him to choose his country.

The first time my grandfather crossed the India-Pakistan border was that winter of 1947, when he departed the country of his birth for what had just become northern Pakistan as a cadet in the first officer-training group of the newly formed Pakistan Army. The last time he crossed was in the winter of 2007, with me.

•

The past is present at Wagah-Attari, on the border between India and Pakistan. Soldiers with bristling, bushy mustaches face each other across barbed-wire fences and iron gates. Every evening, Pakistani soldiers clad in black shalwar kameez and Indian soldiers in their khaki uniforms battle each other in a contest of wills. Hundreds of Indians and Pakistanis visit this checkpoint every day—a mere thirty-minute drive from my home in Lahore—to watch the soldiers strut and twirl their rifles, stamp their metal-edged boots, shout and spray spit at each other, and finally race to fold the flags fluttering above them all day. This tableau is repeated again and again, the revelry belying its bloody history. When violence erupts at the Kashmir border and tensions rise, the tableau is temporarily suspended. More recently, Pakistan returned a captured Indian pilot at Wagah, after an air fight over Kashmir.

I stand under a wide brick arch one cold morning in 2007. Later in the day, loudspeakers will blare nationalist songs that grow louder and louder, drowning out the other side of the fence. Seventeen family members, including my grandfather, Saeed, wait their turn at the checkpoint.

The entrance to Pakistan from India reminds me of a castle rampart, white minarets on either side and flat domes along the battlements, pointing to the sky like milky breasts. *Bab-e-Azadi*, "Freedom Gate," flashes above our heads in gold letters as we walk.

Punjab, both east and west of the borderline, is Punjab. Mustard fields, a vast sea of yellow flowers peppered with bobbing farmers' heads, stretch for miles. On an average summer day, Punjab feels like a desert. Driving through the fields, the road expands, flattens, and shines in the heat, a vision of water blossoms into view. Pushing forth to find this water is a lost cause. It recedes farther and farther away.

Today, the winter fog slowly rises to reveal another Punjab, from another world, mere feet away. Gone are the stalls selling flags, and groups of schoolchildren and families thronging the seats at the border. Porters stand in an endless human chain, tossing sacks of onions, dried fruit, and other goods across the boundary. They are adroit, careful not to step over the thick white line marking the other country.

Nana, being a Pakistani military man, a three-star general, was obviously a threat to Indian security, my uncle said. His jokes don't seem to bother my grandfather, who waits calmly as our passports are pored over by disgruntled border officials.

As we cross the border, we pause briefly in no-man's-land. The early morning fog settles down behind us and shrouds *Bab-e-Azadi* in a veil of gossamer. When we finally step onto Indian soil, I expect a cataclysm of some kind, a voice roaring from the heavens. "You are now entering enemy territory!" What I get is an irritable customs official and Gandhi's kindly face smiling from a perch on a sandy archway.

•

Partition holds a strange place in our memory. On the one hand, it was a tragedy, a tearing asunder, a rejection of religious coexistence. On the other hand, it led to the creation of Pakistan, a nation for the persecuted Muslim minority, as I was taught in school. It created my home. I was taught pride in belonging to a country of underdogs. We prevailed against British imperialism and Hindu nationalism, or so we believed.

Tales of the early days of Pakistan, days of hope and courage, of government offices equipped with no pen and paper, of young idealists making do with very little, abounded. Faces of military heroes who fought and died in wars with India plastered our roads, our billboards, and our textbooks.

The story of Partition was much more complex. In August 1947, Cyril Radcliffe, a British official, drew lines through Punjab and Bengal right before the British planned their departure from India. Slowly simmering tensions bubbled up into full-blown violence. Hindus and Sikhs left in Pakistan scrambled across the border to the new state of India, leaving behind their homes, farms, and worldly possessions. Many Muslims made the same migration to the new country of Pakistan. In all directions, these groups engaged in violence, looting, and rape.

A *New Yorker* profile of the German writer W. G. Sebald's work describes the need to be near the past in order to understand cataclysmic events in history. We must go "in search of places and people who have some connection with us, 'on the far side of time.'" My grandfather's generation is our last connection to this crucial moment of history, to a world being erased from our collective memory. In a way, he was part of this erasure. Until we made this journey, I rarely heard narratives of Partition from him.

As we approached the sixtieth anniversary of Partition, my great aunt, through Indian friends, managed to pinpoint their old address in Jalandhar. We excitedly planned our trip there, but Nana was a silent spectator in the proceedings. For Nana, India had changed. He was an estranged returnee, distant and removed. His past belonged to someone else, and his children were simply tourists in a foreign land.

•

The train Nasreen missed on August 9, 1947, never reached its destination. It was bombed around Amritsar. Many trains were attacked on both sides of the border, arriving at their destinations with blood running through the compartments, women's bodies lying prone with their breasts cut off and thrown into gunny sacks, babies hacked to pieces. Yet they persisted and hurtled forth with the dead, perhaps hoping that they would be afforded a decent burial.

My grandmother finally left on August 11, 1947, during the holy month of Ramzan. The stations were prepared for their arrival after the bombing at Amritsar. A pilot engine ran ahead, sending updates over the radio saying all was clear. As they neared Pakistan, the sense of unease was replaced by euphoria. It was the month of fasting, and at each stop during sunrise and sunset, nearby villagers sent pots of food for the weary travelers.

My grandmother is not alive to remember those days. Her sister Safia, who traveled with her, recalls how their hearts swelled with fervor and empathy as they approached Pakistan. Under a sky marred by smoke, Safia watched others on the train open their fasts and pray. They made it to Karachi on August 13, 1947, the day before Pakistan was born.

I recently discovered a picture of my grandmother, taken exactly a year after she arrived in Pakistan. She stands in front of a group of women and soldiers on the tarmac of Karachi airport. They greet Jinnah, the founder of Pakistan, who has just landed. Jinnah is half-smiling; his hand is raised in salute but his cheekbones are sharply visible; he is dangerously thin. My grandmother is frowning against the sun. Barely a month after this picture was taken, Jinnah would be rushed to a hospital in an ambulance, which would subsequently break down amid

Karachi's heat and traffic. He would breathe his last there and the young country would be thrown into turmoil.

My family's proximity to history, their close shave with tragedy, often colors their perception of Pakistan. Their world is defined by good fortune, a stark difference from the majority who suffered immeasurably before, during, and after Partition. Where I view the past with curiosity, they look back proudly before moving on with their days.

•

The morning fog lifts to reveal fields that look suspiciously like the ones we left behind. I blink a few times, not sure if I am back in my Punjab. I have entered an alternate reality, a mirror of home. Small differences clear the air. India the concept is now the country. The newness and oldness of it overwhelms me.

Turbaned Sikh men work in the fields. Their long beards drag across the crops as they bend over their work. Some have even artfully divided their beards into two sections and tucked one over either shoulder. The billboard signs are different. Gone are the long, elegant Urdu letters in Nastaliq; in their place are rounded, blossoming Gurmukhi and Devanagari scripts. I see a smattering of Urdu on the white stones welcoming us to new cities. Hooks and straight lines cut through each unknown word, and the quick curves race past our eyes as our bus hurtles deeper into a new Punjab.

Jalandhar is now a bustling, noisy, and run-down city that

produces sports goods. Nana marvels at the roads. We cross thousands of buses and motorbikes, potholes, ditches, manufacturing plants, garages, and sports stores selling cricket bats, hockey sticks, and balls.

We are not prepared for our hotel's welcome. The manager stands excitedly with a photographer and a reporter from a local daily. Half a dozen men bound forward to shake hands with Nana as if welcoming a celebrity. Nana, with a bemused smile, wonders aloud what brought them here, and they laugh and say, "You, sir!"

"Sir, we are so excited to welcome you back with your wonderful family."

Our Indian contacts alerted the owners of Jalandhar's daily newspaper about the rare arrival of a large group of Pakistanis. Jalandhar, a town often disregarded by tourists, was once home to many Muslims who crossed over to Pakistan. Muslims still live here, we are told, but Nana's former neighborhood is now largely a Hindu one.

The next day, our bus driver hands a newspaper to my uncle with a flourish. Our smiling faces look up at us under indecipherable script. "What does it say?" my uncle asks.

"Dharti da puttar ghar aa gaya hai." *Son of the soil returns home.*

•

Nana is pensive, overcome by the chatter around him, cocooned by the largeness of our family, which leaves little room for reflection and silence. He is like a new student, aware that this Jalandhar is no longer his Jalandhar. This belongs to another, an alien Saeed who once ran through these streets chasing his kites, and getting into fights with his elder brother.

Our guide is a young Sikh man who invites us to his home, where his wife waits with a feast of pakoray, samosay, and tea. She engages my maternal grandmother in a serious conversation, where much to my consternation I hear her lament her inability to conceive a child. My grandmother asks about her contraception. The sudden familiarity, the immediate bond catches me off guard.

Our hostess looks at my family gathered around their plastic-covered coffee table and exuberantly proclaims in Punjabi, "Tussi saray bauhat sundar ho!" *All you [Pakistanis] are so beautiful!*

My grandmother, not to be outdone, retorts, "Twadey kul tau Aishwarya Rai hai!" *But you have Aishwarya Rai!* (A popular, beautiful Indian actress.) I cringe.

But our hostess beams, pushes her long braid back, and gives what my grandmother considers the ultimate compliment: "Twadey te har kudi Aishwarya Rai hai." *But all your girls are like Aishwarya Rai.*

The compliments continue for a while, each person trying to outdo the other, building to a crescendo until it is time to leave. My grandmother promptly invites her new best friend to Pakistan.

•

We follow a narrow waterlogged lane, surrounded by a smattering of bare, gnarled trees. Dense colonies of houses are clumped together in the distance and heavy fog shrouds the sky. Upon closer inspection, we see newer structures, simple, square brick homes alongside the older houses with wooden doors with intricate carvings almost hanging off their hinges.

Today, the Sikh temple and graveyard still stand, serving as the best markers to find Haveli Nabi Noor, the mansion of Nabi Noor, named for my grandfather's grandfather, my grandparents' birthplace. The lanes get smaller, and the potholes larger. The houses are built tightly together, with high walls in narrow alleyways.

We take a number of sharp turns before our guide pauses at a tall building with a wooden door bordered with intricate flower carvings. Most of the carvings have faded away, but faint Persian inscriptions stand out just above the door. A large brick archway with half of a Quranic verse painted above is also visible. We stare at the door and the familiar script.

I glance at Nana, and see his face brighten. His gaze moves up and down the door.

We knock, and a disheveled young girl with a child hanging on her shirt peers out. She is surprised to see such a large group. Our guide speaks to her, tells her where we are from, and she smiles and lets us in, inviting us to walk around the house. We step into a courtyard with high walls surrounded by stairs that lead up to a roof bordered with arches. A number of Hindu families reside in separate rooms around the courtyard, rooms that are small and dark, with dusty floors and old, creaking doors. Small heads peek through the arches on the rooftop, grinning at us. Another older man and lady greet us shyly. They say we can look around for as long as we like.

Nana, after glancing around the courtyard with a sad smile, climbs the stairs to the roof. I find him looking over a small drop onto a lower platform.

Flat rooftops of varying heights are grouped around the house like a mismatched pile of bricks. Nana pulls off his spectacles and rubs his eyes with his handkerchief. When he lowers his hands, I glimpse a hint of tears, but he is smiling.

My mother turns to Nana with concern. "Abbu, are you all right?"

"I just remembered something," he says. "I remembered my brother and I were flying kites on this roof once. Waheed pushed me and I fell there." Nana points to the lower level, a few feet below.

"I remember I hurt my head quite badly, I was bleeding right there. Waheed was horrible, he laughed at me and our mother . . . she was furious." His eyes widen, his face breaks into a large smile, and he laughs. "She was so angry, she even shouted at me. She hated it when we flew kites up here. I sat under a water tap and cried as someone washed away the blood. I got no sympathy."

Nana continues laughing. His eyes, normally so small and wrinkled around the edges, are large and bright. I have never seen him laugh and cry at the same time. My mother smiles and grasps his arms before leading him back down the steep stairs.

Across the rooftops, the sun darts through rising fog and more houses come into view. Nana starts chatting with the older residents of the house. He asks them how the neighborhood has changed over the years, the names of each lane. Outside the door, he looks up at his grandfather's name.

Eventually, we bid the families in Haveli Nabi Noor farewell. I keep looking back at the old house, before we turn a corner and it vanishes from view. Nana is deep in conversation with our guide; he doesn't look back.

•

A few Indian soldiers at Wagah grin and wave, and I smile back. They look as large as our soldiers, who we often joked are stronger than their Indian counterparts. Perhaps because I have never seen the Indian soldiers up close. They prepare their rifles as they wait for the ceremony to commence.

I want to watch my home from the other side of the border, observe the ceremony from behind enemy lines, but we are hustled through the green-and-white gates before it begins.

Before I can blink, I am back on home territory. Once again, a veil drops over India. Even the music seems muted as we step over the white line and familiar sights and sounds settle back within us. Nana had shrugged off the moment soon after we stepped out of Haveli Nabi Noor. He hugged each of us, looked around with shining eyes, before resuming his cheerful demeanor. I pester him frequently, asking him if he will ever go back.

Why should I? he says often. It's in the past; it was a nice visit. I got to see it all once, and I am happy.

I remember a small moment, however. Across from Haveli Nabi Noor sat a simple, square brick structure. We glanced at it as we left.

"That used to be a house," Nana said. "Nasreen was born right where that brick structure sits."

We stared at the sad, lonely structure. Nothing of the past remained there. A few dried-up trees surrounded it, but there was no address, no mark of anything to indicate that once a little girl, who narrowly escaped death only to have it claim her later, took her first breath here.

Indeed, we had been lucky that Haveli Nabi Noor was still standing. But right now, as he crosses the border back to Pakistan, Nana is not weighed down by these thoughts as we walk to the parking lot. He is laughing, flanked by his grandchildren, and he does not turn around.

Undocumented Lovers

in America

Krystal A. Sital

Submerged in the depths of the pizzeria's kitchen during the hottest month of the year, I wait for the new chef to pass me the plates of food. His brown skin glistens, and his hair, damp from sweat, begins to curl at the nape of his neck. I'm anxious with nothing to take to my tables—checking my watch, tapping my fingers on the countertop, cracking my knuckles. I think, *Why ring the damn bell if the food isn't ready yet?*

I walk back to the wooden door framing a window that looks out into the dining room. My customers are grumbling to one another. I make a mental checklist: Table one needs chicken francese, table two needs veal cacciatore and fried calamari, table nine hasn't even ordered yet, and a line is forming at the door.

I hear another cook call this new guy Juan. A crown of curls quivers beneath his cap as he moves from pan to pan. With an expert flick of his wrist, he arches white wine into a pan. He abandons the emerald-green bottle next to the stove, leaving smudged fingerprints along its neck. Droplets of wine and oil spark and dance along vaporized fumes of diffused alcohol. Again he flicks his wrist and tosses the sauce up; it splashes neatly back into the pan. The sharp scent of lemon cuts through the air. I've watched the other cooks maneuver this kitchen for years but something about his movements mesmerizes me.

"I don't have all day to wait here," I say, trying to break my trance. "Next time ring the bell when it's ready, not when you've just started to cook the food." The other cooks snicker. Juan's back is to me when I say this. He pours the sauce speckled with parsley and oregano over linguine and places it on the partition separating us. The plate teeters on a tin of butter. We reach in to grab it. The plate is hot. Heat jolts me. Sauce spills on my hands. Almost dropping the plate, he catches it. I don't pull my hands back as he wipes the sauce off with his fingers.

When I look up I see lidded eyes underneath a beat-up hat. His forehead is permanently creased from furrowing. He leans forward some more and I see his eyes are the color of warmed honey. His lashes are thick and black, curled back from his eyes.

"Estas bien, Krystal?"

I nod and look down, afraid to fall into the sticky warmth of his gaze again. My hands are cupped in his. Salmon hisses in a pan nearby; spices tickle my nostrils. I hear the chomp of a knife dicing carrots. Pots and pans clang in the sink. His fingers are shiny from butter, oil, and wine. They are thick and rough from years of cooking. I feel people beginning to stare, so I start pulling my hands away, but not before he caresses me once more with his calloused fingers. The tenderness of his brush stays with me long after I've walked away.

Throughout the night, my phone vibrates in my pocket. It's my boyfriend, Michael. In direct contrast to Juan's brooding features, Michael's Irish complexion lights up my screen, crystalline blue eyes piercing mine.

After three years of being his girlfriend, I'd recently told Michael about my undocumented status in America as we stood in an empty parking lot during a walk through town, tormented by the lies burgeoning between us. He dropped my hands and stepped away from me. He sat on a stone divider and raked his hands through his hair and down his face, leaving red lines on his white cheeks. The minutes passed with his heavy sighs between us.

"But you're working on it, right? I mean, it'll be fixed eventually?" He was still sitting away from me.

"I'm not sure, Michael. It's been eight or nine years at this point, I just don't know. We get status updates from immigration but nothing has changed really."

"Okay. I mean, if we were to get married and everything, you'll be legal by then, right?"

"I don't know."

"How will I explain this to my family?"

"Please don't tell anyone anything. You must understand this doesn't only affect me. It's my whole family—my dad, my mom, my sister. I'm trusting you with this secret. I've never told anyone before."

It was true. I'd chosen to lose good friends rather than divulge my family's precarious situation. I continued to plead with him not to tell anyone, especially not anyone in his family. But Michael went home and told his mother anyway, the same woman who, upon meeting me, told her son behind my back I was too dark for him, the same woman who pushed her son away when he leaned in for a kiss one day on returning from one of our family barbecues and said, "You smell like curry. Get away from me, Michael." This same woman had told him he couldn't bring me inside their house while we were dating; she told him she preferred it if we stayed on the front porch where she wouldn't have to see me.

I'd avoided seeing him since then, and that was a week ago. Something had shifted between us. I had somehow taken on an inferior role in our relationship—he got irritated if I questioned him and became vicious when I expressed my displeasure at him telling his family. His brother was a lawyer, so I was worried about what they would do with this information— if his family would wield it against me. There was no room for anger, only concern.

"I only told my mom," he assured me, "and I told her not to tell anyone else."

"Because I have every reason to trust your mom, Michael? The woman doesn't even like me!"

And that was where we left it, so when my phone vibrates again tonight, I shut it off. I walk away from Juan, fighting the urge to look back at him. I allow the heavy plates to ground me. Yet all I see around me are his tired eyes infused with a spark of interest. The shine of his skin, the blue flames ringed yellow, the heat, the black, the white, all push and pull me into the kitchen. The dishes warm my hands. I kick open the door with my right foot and the cool breeze of the air conditioner ices my sweat.

I couldn't have known he didn't ring the bell that day, that he bit his lip when he flicked the sauce and some splattered his skin, nor seen the tremble of his hands as he set the plates out. I did what people inexplicably do after time—I saw what I wanted to see.

I did not, however, feel what I wanted to feel. Each time I entered the kitchen and he was there, his breath drew with mine, he captured my gaze as I did his, and I always welcomed the touches he offered. Amid the rolling boils of pasta and the popping of tomatoes bursting in the pots, I looked forward to his lingering stares. I held the tickets up for him to read.

"Table three wants fried calamari, clams, and mussels," I told him.

He wrapped his fingers around mine, raising the ticket between us. He looked not at the ticket but into my eyes.

"Sí, Krystal," he said, rolling the *r* in my name in the most decadent way possible.

I always walked away smiling, a familiar spin of emotions spiraling down my torso. I'd begun to neglect Michael, filling my days with twelve-hour work schedules whenever I wasn't taking classes, so I could see Juan whenever I wanted. On the days I signed up to work all day and he wasn't there, the disappointment that dwelled within me ran as deep as the ocean.

He whispered questions to me and I moved in closer to answer them, enjoying the way his eyes played upon my body. Sometimes I sat next to him while he cooked. We joked and laughed. When he moved closer to me, I rested my head on his shoulder. The smell of stale oil mixed with his cologne wafted off him. The cooks in the kitchen turned away or averted their eyes while our hands found each other's under the counter.

One day he placed his hand over his chest and said, "Ay, Krystal, tengo dolor en mi corazón."

"Your heart hurts? What happened?"

From inside his shirt, he pulled out a single white rose, thorns stippled like fine hairs along the stem.

"For me?"

"Sí, para ti, Krystal."

With upturned palms, he presented the rose. Though attractive when covered in butter and oil, his hands, before work, were cracked and dry. Caked with grime, the ridges of his nails and skin were blackened and tainted. I yearned to rub life back into them.

Abandoning the dining room when it wasn't busy, I stayed in the kitchen, where I helped him rinse rice. We submerged our hands in the water, our fingers sifting the grains. I helped him pry lustrous mussel shells apart, knead dough, and pound meat. I told him I had a boyfriend. He told me about his girlfriend in Mexico. These revelations deterred neither of us, the comfort of two brown bodies lost in America succumbing to the tantalizing aromas of food.

At eleven at night, the pizzeria shut down and the boss

arrived to collect the money for the day. That meant no fraternizing with the guys in the back. I packed up the pepperoni rolls, garlic knots, and calzones from the front. I wiped down the figurines of fat pizza men spinning dough and the bottles of olive oil, vinegar, and pepper seeds.

Covered in dried pizza sauce and grease, I untied my apron. Still talking about her daughter, the boss lady beckoned me to the car. I muttered something about the bathroom and disappeared in the back one last time to find him. But he wasn't there.

"I don't need a ride tonight," I said emerging from the kitchen. Though this was my answer every night, it was nice of her to offer. The girls working there thought I was one of them—another college girl waitressing on the side. They didn't know this job was a lifeline for me, that it was the only work I could get that paid off the books, no questions asked.

A few blocks away from work, I saw Juan smoking a cigarette on the corner. It was the first time I'd seen him outside the walls of our job. Months of our games had slipped away. His hat was off, his head full of ringlets shining in the silver moonlight. Curlicues of smoke danced around his head.

"Ay, Krystal," he said as I drew closer. "Estas muy bonita, chiquita."

I'd learned enough Spanish over the years to enjoy the compliment. His workman fingers moved through my hair, tickled my scalp, sifted my hairs as though memorizing every strand. The heat from our bodies was overpowering. I inhaled the familiar smells of food. His arms circled my waist, his hands squeezed my thighs. I trembled, shook, quaked. I'd begun to unravel.

Closing my eyes, I fell into him, two people with illegal status from two different parts of the world melding together momentarily.

•

That was the beginning.

Soon, I was as familiar with his living space as I was with mine—his bare attic room on the third floor of a lopsided house. We entered one day by way of rickety back steps and one fire escape ladder. He explained how he rented this room from a friend and didn't want to interrupt their family time on the floor below.

"How old is their little girl?" I asked.

"En español, Krystal."

"Fine," I said. "Cuantos años tiene su hija?"

"Cinco."

My Spanish, good before, was now excellent because of him. He now spoke to me only in Spanish, and though my responses were sometimes shaky, we'd shifted from English almost entirely.

I stood by the window as he shrugged off his sweater and hung it inside an old wardrobe next to us. He flicked on a lamp sitting atop a broken table next to his bed and weak light pulsed around the shade. The threadbare carpet beneath my sneakers was stained. Compared to my apartment, where my parents had worked so hard to make it feel like home—my mom painting the walls, gluing decorative wallpaper, and sewing curtains; and my dad tiling the bathroom, making new cupboards for the kitchen, and running wires for new lights—Juan's meager surroundings screamed desolation, utter loneliness. Everything I witnessed was what I felt inside.

"Who's this?" I asked him even though I suspected it was his girlfriend. There was a picture of a woman on a CD case. Her short bleached hair was flipped out onto her shoulders. Her eyes were lidded like his but her gaze was intense, severe, her lips pressed into a line.

"Karina," he whispered, his voice hoarse and low. The way his voice caressed her name sent a warning through me but I pushed it to the side. I didn't want to deal with that then, not when forging a connection with someone like me was so close, just within my grasp.

In the months that followed, that attic floor became as familiar to me as my own bedroom. I lied to my boyfriend, Michael, ignored the few friends I had, saw no one but Juan and the inside of his room. They couldn't understand the shadows I existed in, always lying, living in fear.

If I were to get caught doing anything, my family could get deported. Something as simple as supplying identification so I could get a drink in a bar required me to walk around with my passport and explain to everyone, "Sorry, lost my ID and haven't had a chance to replace it yet," but that could only work for so long. My friends would get a slap on the wrist, just a warning, and their families would be fine.

Juan lived with the same fears I did every day. But I never told him that. I couldn't trust anyone with that information for fear of how they could use it against me.

Tangled in bedsheets one day, he asked me to marry him.

"Para documentos," he clarified.

Not for love. For papers. He didn't know the one reason that drove me to him, the one thing that united us, the one thing no one else around us could understand—our lack of legal status in the United States. While Juan was surrounded by other Mexicans like him in the kitchen of the pizzeria, all of them undocumented, I had to pretend. He had a community of people who shared his background, culture, and fears, while I had no one. He thought the girl he was bedding was an American citizen, a girl foolish enough to marry him and give him the status we both so desperately craved.

He asked again and again, and after he realized my answer would always be no, he turned to drinking more. The six-packs he often brought home with him turned into twelve-packs that he drained one right after the other, bottles clinking as he tossed them into a pile. I'd gotten used to joining him too, enjoying the numbing effect alcohol often had on my senses.

Drunk, I no longer cared that Michael and I were always fighting, and I ignored the phone calls Juan always slipped away to take when I was with him. I had become this young woman who cheated instead of telling the truth and breaking away; I lied to my family every time I slipped away telling them I was working when what I was doing was lying in the bed of a man who was using me more than I was him. Who was this person I had become? Could I crawl out of it? Did I want to?

I stopped drinking with him and, equipped with sharper senses and all my emotions, I started to ask questions about the phone calls he took out on the fire escape every night.

"Who are you talking to?"

"Mi hija, Krystal," and he caressed my name in the long, lazy way he often did, his voice calling forth something deep in me. But, no longer drunk, I continued pestering him.

"If it's your daughter, why are you outside in the dead of winter talking to her? Why not in here with me?"

He just ignored me, turned his back, and slipped out the window with a bottleneck hooked between his fingers. I sat by the window and strained to hear what he said.

"Karina . . . mi amor . . . mi vida . . . te amo mi amor . . . Voy a volver por tí."

An unfounded hatred of a woman I wronged started to seep through me. She was his everything, his love, his life; he revered her among all others, and he was going to return to her and only her. What was I thinking, allowing myself to become infatuated with this man eleven years older than me? Why couldn't I stop myself from hating her? She was the mother of his daughter.

When he slid in through the window, he cupped his hands to his mouth and puffed warm air into them.

"Ay, Krystal, qué pasó?"

No chiquita. Nothing. Just what was wrong?

"Nada, Juan. Nada."

I knew about Karina but she didn't know about me. I realized I was a way to pass his time in America until he could return to Mexico and be with his family. While I cherished the time I spent with him and imagined a deeper bond existed between us, I was a story he told to the friends he trusted and who snickered behind my back.

Anger flashed in his eyes as he moved toward me. I was yelling too much; the family downstairs would hear me, and he didn't want to explain me to them.

"Karina," he said while looking at me. And then he stopped, realizing his mistake. "Krystal, lo siento, it was a mistake. Nothing else."

In my rage, I couldn't understand I was doing the same to him except no child was at stake. I felt used and betrayed, flashes of me slipping into Michael's car moments after Juan's beard has scratched my body raw, taking control of my actions. I shoved Juan against the wall.

"Krystal," he begged.

But I wanted no more of it.

I thought of Michael clambering on top of me, my insides still slick from Juan's touch, his moans still in my ear, reminding myself to say the right name, to moan in English.

What kind of person had I become? How could I do this to someone else?

"No," I screamed.

I stormed down the precipitous staircase that led to the apartment below. I was leaving the way I should have always entered and left, not only the select times Juan knew the family wasn't home or had already gone to bed. Startled, the woman and the little girl looked up at my tear-stained face. I flew through the door and into the cold night, buttoning up my thin jacket.

It was late. The turmoil that filled me was a stark contrast to the eerily quiet night. I looked behind me but he hadn't followed. I started walking in the direction of my apartment but was unsure I could make the thirty-seven blocks home in the dead of winter wearing nothing but a glorified sweater. Torn, I kept checking behind me, a part of me hoping he was following to make sure I was safe and another thinking he should stay as far away from me as possible. Though I checked my phone often, it remained silent.

In the days that followed, I approached my studies with renewed vigor, determined to finish up my last year and a half of college. We couldn't be together; I'd known that all along, but I wanted it to be untrue. He was the first person I could move through life with. I understood him on such an intimate level; his stories of crossing from Mexico and into America were both frightening and appealing. But we didn't share common ground, because even though he shared his secrets with me, I kept my secrets from him, protecting myself and my family as I'd always done.

We fell into each other a few times after that but it was no longer the same. His voice no longer captivated me, the lines on his face had lost their intrigue, the stories I found in the scars on his body belonged to someone else. It wasn't fair of me to cause another woman this pain.

When he disappeared from the kitchen of the restaurant, I thought he was sick, but days and weeks passed by before I realized he'd returned to Mexico. On my walks home at night, even though I didn't want to, I saw him leaning against the tree we always rendezvoused under after work, cap pulled over his curls, smoke disappearing around his head. I found him in the shadows, one foot resting against the trunk of a tree. But when I moved closer there was no one there. I heard him in the scrape of the branches against one another—Krystal—the way only he said my name, the way it should be pronounced, he often said.

A month after he left, my phone rang and his breath over the phone brought back everything I'd been holding at bay.

"Wait for me," he said. "I'll come back for you."

They were the same words he whispered to Karina. He wanted us both, the loneliness here wrecking him while he was away from her. Maybe now, while in Mexico, he thought of me, saw my eyes in hers, forced himself to say her name instead of mine.

I now wanted none of it—neither him nor Michael—but untangling myself from the mess I'd created would take time.

In the little room I shared with my sister, I sat at the simple desk my parents scrounged together to buy for me, this space my only solace. I understood now that my sanctuary lay in the messy sheaf of handwritten and typed sheets splayed across its surface, and also within the pages of my modest collection of used books. I breathed deeply. Our papers for legal residency were in the works, had been for years, and I needed to trust that my grandmother's sponsorship of our family would eventually be approved. In the meantime, I would return to school, to writing, with renewed vigor. Uncapping the nib of my worn fountain pen, I wrote, staining the white pages before me the color of the Caribbean sea.

Say It with Noodles

Shing Yin Khor

At the temple where my grandmother's ashes rest, we offer her —

oranges for our good fortune

a cup of tea

and steamed buns, because she liked them.

THE INCENSE SMELLS LIKE JASMINE.

HER KITCHEN SMELLED LIKE FRYING OIL.

My grandmother and I didn't speak the same language.

Not really. Not enough.

I am not part of an emotionally demonstrative family. How could we be, when my first language was their fourth language?

But my grandmother cooked.

Her kitchen was a wet kitchen. The floor was concrete and usually damp.

My dad says that his family was quite poor, but I didn't know it.

How would I have known? There was always so much food.

I have no memory of my grandmother telling me she loved me.

But of course I knew.

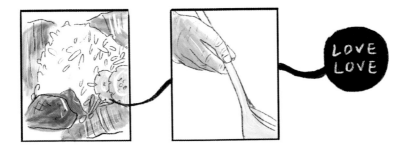

I made breakfast for someone who had wronged me, and it felt bad. Feeding someone I hate is a lie.

My favorite are our large meals.

We maneuver past each other, coordinating stove top space and wooden spoons, knowing when to step back.

The kitchen is our temple.

Our spices are hymns; our knives holy relics.

Dishwashing is a necessary ritual.

hey! FOOD'S READY!

and we eat together.

Even as I learned how to speak with food, I still ate the same thing for lunch everyday.

A packet of ramen.

I justified it as a cheap meal, but that was not true.

The truth was, I did not feel worthy of my own care.

YOU THINK COOKING MAKES PEOPLE LIKE YOU. THAT'S CUTE.

I have a complicated relationship with food.

If I claim food as one of my languages, I have to acknowledge that you can say many things with a language.

you are so ugly.

you are such a slob.

you eat alone because no one likes you.

I wish I could articulate better, how I learned to speak love to myself, but I know some of it is this—

I can find peace in ritual.

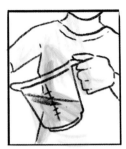

If I cannot love myself with nourishment, I can love myself with labor.

I can find peace in my stack of small ceramic prep bowls, gifted by dear ones, and acquired from my travels.

Onions make me cry, and it feels good.

I feel strong when I lift my five quart Dutch oven.

My Grandmother's Patois and Other Keys to Survival

Sharine Taylor

"Which aisle has the soup packs?" my grandmother asked the shopping attendant. I noticed all her words were perfectly enunciated. The soft Patois that often gripped her tongue was replaced by a more palatable, less judgmental English. The attendant led us to the soup packs and my grandmother's brown eyes scanned the rack for the cock-flavored mix. She was getting ready to prepare a dish that she had been making since she was a child: her most coveted chicken soup.

"Oh, thank you so much!" she said with a smile. Once the attendant was out of sight, she picked up two packs and threw them into her shopping basket, kissing her teeth. "Yuh no this ah get more expensive," she said, slipping back into her more familiar way of speaking. It was not a question. It was a definitive statement coded as a question, but I was used to the way she disregarded the conventions of speech in exchange for her own.

When I was growing up, my grandmother's sly remarks in Patois provided the comedic relief when we went out. Patois was our secret, allowing us to be in the English world and then escape to Jamaica through language—if only for brief moments at a time.

A ritual followed her speech, in which I would laugh loudly, too loudly, and she'd hush me up and pinch me with a smirk. That's how our times out would go: English in public, Patois in private.

•

My grandmother was born fourteen years before Jamaica received its independence. The colonial oversight that had controlled the island loosened, but she would still grapple with its insidious residue through her speech, even when she was 1,776 miles away.

She migrated to Toronto, Canada, in 1971. Prior to her arrival, Canada had just received part of its second wave of Caribbean immigrants through the West Indian Domestic Scheme, a policy implemented in 1955. The need for domestic labor in a postwar Canada afforded a select group of Caribbean women—particularly from Jamaica and Barbados—who were single, aged eighteen to thirty-five, had at least an eighth-grade education, and successfully passed an interview and medical examination with Immigration Canada, an opportunity to get permanent residency and increased likelihood of sending for their families in exchange for one year of domestic labor. My grandmother saw an opportunity for herself. Arriving with one suitcase, fifty Canadian dollars, and a desire for a better way of living, she settled in the West Toronto neighborhood of (pre-gentrified) Trinity Bellwoods, preparing for my then three-year-old mother, who was back in Jamaica, to join her.

My grandmother was able to build a comfortable life for herself in her new home: She started doing precarious house-keeping work until she was able to secure a stable job, dedicated her life to serving God, and was able to accumulate all that was needed to change her socioeconomic status—a much different reality than the country life in Trelawny, Jamaica, that was the backdrop to her youth. She had done all she needed to do to effectively assimilate into this new life, but once she opened her mouth, her tongue would reveal her otherness.

Because of this, she reserved Patois for intimate spaces, particularly the church and our home. Four a.m. was her des-ignated prayer time, and not a morning went by when I wasn't awakened by her cries to Christ. She thanked Him for her life and pleaded to Him to repair the bad in the world, in our fam-ily, or in her personal life. Her words for the early morning were lazy but still purposeful, a contrast to her quick and witty replies, which we frequently giggled about. The denouement to her spiritual appeals would be eclipsed with hymns she had sung throughout her Christian life. "When you see mi go pon God business, Satan move, mek mi pass." She sang her Patois, evoking more conviction and rigor with each new line.

This would continue throughout the week until Sunday morning, when we made our way to church. Our congregation was composed of people from different countries within the Caribbean, including a strong number of older Jamaican folks. Part of my formative memories of Patois were made here, amid the elders who would give us peeks into their youth through their storytelling and my pastor who, at the height of her sermon, would sometimes slip into the lexicon that we all knew. We sang hymns, said prayers, lifted our voices, and received revivals weaving in and out of the languages of our three worlds: English, Patois, and tongues.

Church would end six hours later, as very Pentecostal and very Caribbean churches do. Youth would run to the back room for patties and pastries, and adults would engage in pleasantries. Everyone would go back to their lives, likely shedding their Patois upon exiting, to engage with the world in Standard English, and inadvertently replicating the relationship that people had with Patois back home.

·

The sound of Jamaican Patois will forever be my favorite song. It's as expressive and sharp as the people who speak it, but its history is one informed by the country's colonial past. Then slave owners forced slaves to speak English, outlawing their native tongue. What was left was a fragmented English, whose vernacular has etymological roots in British, African, and Asian languages, reflecting the diversity of the country's people.

But the politics of Patois have limited how it's regarded

both on and off the island. It hasn't been recognized as the country's official language. Whether or not it is a dialect or language is a catalyst for debate. And its employment is sometimes seen as a marker of class and socioeconomic status, typically reserved for the country's lower-class or rural citizens.

Decades later, my grandmother still contends with this through her veiled Patois and strategic usage of English. In her new world, she knew she would be subject to criticism already, and chose to speak "properly." The minute her Patois fell in the ears of others, her black body would be scripted as one that did not belong—as one belonging to an immigrant and uneducated, among other things.

.

When my grandmother and I get together now, I'm usually met with a speech about how I don't see her as frequently as I used to before getting older and assuming more responsibilities of my own, but I'm always embraced with a hug and many kisses. No matter how much time stands between our last and current encounter, I look forward to traveling to her days in Jamaica through her stories. My favorite stories are the ones from when she was very young.

She was given the nickname "Bad Penny" for how often she misbehaved. In one instance, my great-grandmother sent her to the market to buy mangoes. On her way home, she began to get hungry, so she decided to suck out the fruit and juice from one end of the mango and replace its insides with small pebbles. When her mother found out, she was, understandably, not impressed. My grandmother and I cackle at the thought of her getting away with it.

Storytelling has a way of transporting you to another place, bringing you along on a visceral journey. When my grandmother tells the stories of her past, I see her revert back to her most vulnerable self. Her wrinkled hands make grand gestures and her face explodes with expression. I'm always drawn into how she's able to re-create voices and locations through her words, reminding me in these moments that this is a much older Bad Penny—whose story is illustrated by the vibrancy of Patois.

In the spaces I occupy now, I think about the ways of communicating I have at my disposal. How I unapologetically take up space with language, embedding Patois in my academic writing; how I am often afforded the opportunity to speak Patois in Toronto, among the many other Jamaican migrants and first- and second-generation children.

I do this for my grandmother. For all the times she made a decision to draw from her secondary bank of knowledge in an effort to conceal her difference. For all the times she sacrificed showcasing the beauty of her language to quell the curiosity of others. For all the times she's thought of me and my future, I think I think about her and her past.

THE DRESS

Soraya Membreno

I do not own any soft, pretty white dresses. I probably never will. Every time I spot one, all I can think is, *That could have been the Dress.*

If you're a young woman in her early twenties graduating from a certain kind of tiny, elite liberal arts college in the Northeast, the graduation dress represents a rite of passage. A carryover from the boarding school past shared by many students, it is a very specific kind of dress, a white or cream-colored or pale pastel shift, simple and strapless.

Coming from a public school in Miami, the graduation dress was a tradition I did not learn about until it was too late—until I was standing in line, in alphabetical order, wearing a too bright, too casual, not particularly flattering red-and-white-polka-dotted "Minnie Mouse dress" (as my mother later dubbed it, when looking through the handful of pictures my father managed to take that day). In the middle of that brick courtyard, surrounded by buildings older than the country from which my parents had fled, I remember feeling thankful for the weight and length of our thick black commencement gowns; for the way mine hid all traces of unintentional Disney-infused childhood nostalgia on the day I was supposed to be coming into my adulthood.

•

My first day at college was nothing like what TV had promised me. There was no carefully packed minivan or raucous family escort into the chaotic, half-empty cement dorms. Instead, I hopped on a plane in Miami with a single suitcase and a backpack and arrived on campus alone, before the rest of the student body, for a pre-orientation program designed to give first-generation students time to adjust before everyone else flooded in. My first day there was a quiet one, spent neatly unpacking my belongings and then taking a bus to the nearest Walmart to get the rest of the things I needed. While most incoming students were trailed by parents fussing over their twin XL sheets and lack of shower shoes, I went about my to-do list on my own.

My last day of college was nothing like what I'd expected, either. There was no first-generation orientation for commencement weekend; no one to prepare me for the jarring collision of the home my dad brought with him and the bubble I'd spent four years building; no instructions for the day I learned, suddenly and grotesquely, that the American ideal of upward mobility is a solo mission.

In a way, it came as a relief to me when the weekend was pitched to us as a time for friends rather than family. There were dozens of school-sanctioned parties and seniors-only events; an entire week was devoted to a road trip to Hilton Head for our last drunken hurrah before returning to campus to do more of the same, in nicer clothes. But I had either forgotten, or was never prepared for, the descent of the New England elite upon the campus—and how much everything, and everyone, changed in their presence. The old women in sun hats and small children both felt misplaced, but even more startling were my own classmates' transformations. The place where we had lived with our unofficial dress code of black and gray North Face and sweatpants was suddenly overrun with pastel. A different sundress for every day of the week! Beyond the unexpected Easter vibes that left me scrambling in friends' closets, I overheard students talking about accommodations and BBQs, debating where to hold dinner with their friends and family—at the refurbished farmhouse one set of parents had rented for the weekend? Or the cute inn another had bought out for the occasion (which had a pool)?

I had known a few months out that my mother wouldn't be there for my graduation. Stuck between visas and embassies, her absence was explained once and never mentioned again. My dad arrived the day before commencement, in a rental car he drove from Albany an hour away. That night I took him to my favorite restaurant for wings and the novel first beer with his of-age daughter. It was surprisingly easy to find a table for two. He got surprisingly buzzed. And I was taken aback with the discovery of a new, all-consuming, ferocious sense of protectiveness I felt toward my father.

The lone representative from the immediate family nucleus, unable to speak English, he spent the one night he was there tucked away in the farthest corner of the campus, in the freshman dorms the college had set aside for the parents of first-generation and lower-income students (for whom a weekend at a local inn would be "a hardship"). Depositing my father at the opposite end of campus in a threadbare, single-occupancy dorm felt like an almost violent act of separation. He called me about an hour into his stay; he couldn't find the bathroom. Then he got disoriented on his way back to his room. I talked him through it; he made a joke about "experiencing" college, and said good night.

The next morning, waiting in line, I looked at my father in the crowd. I tried to smile at him, but his scanning eyes could not find a place to land in the thicket of gowns. In a suit jacket that hung too loosely from weight he'd lost too quickly, he wandered this unfamiliar place with just a camera for company, mostly taking pictures of trees and the old brick row houses. Smiling, and by all accounts having the time of his life, but still . . . the guilt I'd kept at bay for the past four years—for leaving, for not visiting enough, for not sharing this life I was building around me and then springing it on him in the span of two days, right at the end—made him difficult to look at.

My father is nothing if not a proud, stubborn man. But that day I recalled how, every couple of years, he would decide it was time he learn this language once and for all and sit down with his books and DVDs; how he'd hear the way his tongue strangled the words and, painfully aware of how he must sound to other people, he'd slam the books shut and hide them away again in a quiet corner of the house. This same man was now taking pictures of the most mundane things—the trashed, half-empty dorm; the rental car he had driven up; a pile of books I couldn't take on the plane with me, but refused to get rid of—all to share with my mother, six thousand kilometers away, calling her when he learned some interesting new fact about my school that could not be photographed. His simple joy killed me. For once, he felt no embarrassment; he did not shy away from the words he could not pronounce, but repeated them until he committed them all to memory: names of buildings, and streets, and professors he would never see again.

•

He missed the hand-off of the diploma; he couldn't quite follow the ceremony while trying to narrate it to my mother over the phone. They both heard my name being called, my father standing in the erected bleachers, my mother from the house in Nicaragua—but he said he couldn't see me, couldn't scramble fast enough to get the camera ready.

That day, constantly whisked away to stand in yet another line, for yet another procession, I mostly saw my father from a distance. I had never stood here before, looking at him surrounded by my classmates in their light, misty dresses and khaki pants; had never had a chance to see myself, my family, the way others might. Somewhere along the line, in the flurry of niceties and ceremonies, with my father relegated to the sidelines of my peripheral vision, that weekend made clear the very thing I had been denying for the past four years: I was being subsumed by something else, going to a place where my family could not follow. I stood out like hell, a polka-dotted dress in a sea of white, but there I was, still in it. Still a part of it. And he could do no more than snap a picture.

I wanted to run my father under cover, hide him from this thing he had yet to notice. I knew on some level that he was immensely proud of me, but I also felt, for the first time, the fear of translation and everything that might be lost in it. When everyone spilled onto the lawn after the ceremony, diplomas in hand, posing for pictures, I fled. I grabbed a plate of tiny sandwiches, careful to not get anything on my newly acquired $200,000 piece of paper, and I got my dad out of there—out of a desire to protect or to hide, for his sake or for my own, I still don't know.

•

Thankfully, now, Graduation Day is just a Sunday I try to not think too much about. But it took me about a year to stop obsessively opening emails and magazines from stores I never shopped at in hopes of finding the Dress. If I could at least identify what the right one *would* have been, I kept thinking, maybe I could brush off my outlier of a dress as a choice—some small act of rebellion.

Now, whenever my mother looks at the two or three graduation pictures on my father's computer—because there is no framed portrait or blown-up image hanging on any walls—all the illusions break down. I see the blame spiral start at her eyes, tunneling downward to her gut. I want to tell her that I barely noticed she wasn't there, I was so busy; I want to tell her it's commonplace, just undergrad, just another silly ceremony no one will remember. She hates how few pictures there are from that day, but part of me is thankful for my father's distraction, because that means there is less evidence to tally my mother's absence.

When I think of that day now, I think of oceans and distance and strength; of how different it was from how any of us ever imagined. I point to the dress, and my mom shakes her head.

"Pero, Sorayita," she says, "de verdad ese vestido?"

But she laughs every time.

What Miyazaki's Heroines Taught Me

Nina Li Coomes

One summer day when I was nine, I climbed into a hair stylist's chair and asked them to cut my hair to my ears. Until that point, I'd always had a head of long hair tumbling over my shoulder, useful for coquettish tossing when I imagined myself as Snow White or Cinderella. I had never worn short hair, had never wanted it; I'd always thrived on girliness, which fed into my obsession with imitating what I perceived to be the ultrafeminine Disney princess archetype. But that summer, sitting in a chair too tall for me, I asked the friendly lady with the scissors to take it all. After a moment of thought, I told her, "Short—like a princess raised by wolves."

I was referencing San, from Hayao Miyazaki's *Mononoke-hime*, or *Princess Mononoke*. In the film, San is a human girl left as a sacrifice to the gods of the mountain by her human parents, and raised by the very god to whom she was sacrificed—Moro, a wolflike inugami—and convinced, as a result, that she, too, is a wolf. When the viewer meets San for the first time, her small face is pressed to an open wound in her wolf-mother's flesh. She turns her head toward the viewer, momentarily breaking the fourth wall, her face smeared in bright red. She spits a jet of blackening blood and rubs her fist along the edge of her chin, as if to wipe the stain of blood from her face. The utter humanness of this gesture, paired with her clear physical intimacy with the wolf-god, immediately casts her identity into conflict—a theme to be played over and over throughout the movie. Is San a wolf? Is she a girl? Is she neither, or both, or something in between?

Later in the film, as tensions between humans and gods come to a head, San inadvertently thrusts her small frame into the path of a lumbering boar-god that is consumed with a ropey, steaming, literal manifestation of rage. As she clings to the charging boar, pleading for it to let go of its anger, the tentacular curse begins to root itself in her human skin. She tries to push it off but ultimately fails, disappearing into the hide of the increasingly unrecognizable boar-god, her fragile human figure swallowed by this stark conflict between animal gods and mortal humans—as if the conflict of her own identity has overwhelmed her physicality. Though San is later saved, Miyazaki never supplies an answer as to what she is. She refuses to return to humanity, staying in the woods. It is never clear where her body belongs, or what she is—human or god.

I left the salon with a shapeless bob ending jaggedly just below my ears, just like San's. Later, when I was teased by a classmate that I looked like a boy, I turned around and bit his arm, drawing a thin line of salty blood.

•

When I was seven, my family moved from Nagoya, Japan, to Chicago, though we often returned to spend summers in Japan. The summer I got my hair cut short was two years into my family's residence in the States. Still reeling from our transpacific upheaval, I was happy to return to what once was home, yet had found Japan suddenly tinged with a steely alienness. And that summer, it was not just home that seemed alien to me. My body was beginning to lack familiarity, too, and a slow, cold realization was dawning.

Born significantly underweight, I had always been a long, spindly child. A bundle of elbows and knees, I was constantly tripping, hitting my head, ambling about like a colt learning to walk. I was, by American standards, painfully thin. By Japanese standards I looked identical to my peers. I knew this because of our annual school trip to the bathhouse, where we would all gather around the steaming tub, our bodies present and accountable, held in front of all—all of us with our skin thinning at the ribs, each vertebra visibly poking out of our backs. It didn't matter that I had an American father, or that we spoke a hodgepodge English-Japanese pidgin at home; standing at the bathhouse with my peers, I retained a steadfast assurance in my place among the other children, my bodily equality.

When we moved to the States, I learned that people came in an array of different shapes and sizes. Skin variations of color stretched from peach to taupe to ebony. In the musty basement of a countryside church, I learned I was "yellow," as the children's choir director scolded me for wearing a green shirt, apparently unacceptable for my coloring. The children in my first-grade class also inhabited a catalogue of different bodies, or so I suspected—I could never be sure, since we never took trips to bathhouses. Despite my confusion, I ate American food and adapted to this new American life with new American bodies.

In Miyazaki's Academy Award–winning *Sen to Chihiro no Kami Kakushi* (*Spirited Away*), there is a scene in which the protagonist Chihiro realizes, with creeping dread, that she is in a different world—a world of spirits. She hurtles through streets that once seemed innocuous, now full of shadowy forms. A ghost gestures to her from a window, waving her toward what was once an empty building. She slumps down on a riverbank in despair as she watches a boat pull into a harbor: gods in fantastical forms, man-size chickens and floating approximations of Noh masks, waver on the deck as they wait to cross the gangplank onto land. Gasping, Chihiro brings her hands to her eyes only to discover they are translucent. She is disappearing. She is trapped in a land of gods and ghosts, and now her physical self is vanishing.

Eventually, she is saved by being given a small seed to eat, told that unless she eats something of the spirit world, she will disappear entirely. Chihiro appears hesitant, staring at the red kernel in front of her as if a cognizant Persephone, and finally takes the seed, forcing herself to swallow. Slowly, her body re-appears, solidifying. And yet, now she, like San, exists in an ambiguous in-between: Is she now a spirit in a realm of spirits? Or is her body still that of a human girl?

That summer, I frequented bathhouses similar to those in *Spirited Away* with my mother and sister. One day I stood un-der a showerhead, rinsing my body of dirt and grime before entering the bath, and noticed that the arc of my stomach was jutting softly below my sternum. I had never seen my stomach before, not from this vantage point, with my chin tucked and hair wet. I had always been concave, a pocket of negative space ballooning between my rib cage and hips. To see my stom-ach take up space was new and strange. As I stared, water ran into my eyes and questions churned in my head: What was I becoming? Was I becoming American? Was I not Japanese anymore? Had I ever been Japanese?

A steady, fluttering shame took root in my chest, and I was reminded of the ambiguous existence Chihiro entered when eating the food of the spirit world. By eating the food of a foreign land, I had lost the ability to recognize my own body.

•

My body continued to change in other ways, for other reasons. With the onset of puberty, my hips folded outward, flaring at thighs webbed with stretch marks, tapering into my waist. My arms rounded, but my shoulders stayed small and sloping.

A mixed-race body moving through homogeneous spaces often inspires attempts at conversations of classification. Whether through the form of a sudden, uneasy speechlessness followed by a mumbled comment, or an incessant stream of questions, this body of mine often seems to inspire the same disquietude in others that I experience within myself. In a crowded Tokyo mall, I once found myself the subject of a Japanese man's gaze. When I moved to avoid him, climbing the stairs to the next floor, he positioned himself silently beside me, all the while staring at my face, my posture, my hands, my body. Only when I turned to exit did he open his mouth to mumble, "Jyun-japa?" ("Pure Japanese?"). He lifted his eyes to mine and I felt myself overcome by a blanketing silence.

Last week, in a cab home from Boston's airport, the white woman behind the wheel began playing an all-too-familiar game: "So let me guess—Native American? Mexican? If those are wrong, I'd say maybe Romanian." I was tired, jet-lagged, and emotionally drained from a farewell with my family, but still she insisted on trying to guess my ethnicity. When I finally told her, she said, "I *knew* you must be mixed with white. All the good ones are."

As the questions about what I am and what I represent emerge, I often find myself silenced, unable to give a concise answer. Some mornings, I wake up and feel resigned to mutely inhabit a stranger's skin—like Sophie Hatter of Miyazaki's *Howl's Moving Castle*, who literally wakes one morning in a much older body. Sophie offends a witch and is changed from a young woman into a crone. Instead of falling into despair,

Sophie packs her bags and leaves home. She treks up a craggy hill, bemoaning her newly creaking bones, and stops at the door of a moving castle (in truth more of a mobile junk heap) belonging to the supposedly fearsome magician Howl, infamous for eating the hearts of young, beautiful girls. She supposes now that she is old and ugly, Howl does not pose much of a danger to her, and barges in.

Inhabiting an alien-to-her body, Sophie begins to display a previously alien bravery: She cleans unimaginable messes, lies outright to kings, and even has the audacity to fall in love. It is never clear what part of the enchantment holds her in her elder form, but Miyazaki offers the viewers several hints. For Sophie, part of the witch's curse stipulates that she cannot speak about the curse. Whenever she begins to try to assert the truth of her body, her mouth knits itself together, preventing an overt discussion of her conflicting existence. People around her can ask questions about who she is, where she came from, how she came to be, but she cannot answer them with the truth.

But her inability to speak about her existence is not just tied to the curse. In one scene, Howl gifts Sophie a field of flowers. Gesturing to the never-ending hills of pastel pink blossoms, he turns to Sophie, who stands in front of him in the form of a young woman, as if the curse has been momentarily disarmed. Taken aback, Howl tells Sophie that she is beautiful. Immediately, Sophie denies his compliment, shrinking and folding back into her elderly enchantment. Her insecurity and internal conflict surrounding her physical existence swallow her voice. Even when the curse ceases to exist, Sophie is voiceless.

Throughout the film, Sophie's body exists as yet another female body in flux, presenting a conundrum for the viewer: Is Sophie truly inhabiting the body of a stranger? Or is she still physically herself, somehow fast-forwarded through time? Is the spell cast on her not one of total transformation, but just a catalyst for a phenotypical manifestation of her own doubt and self-denial, a manifestation of her inability to articulate her existence?

•

In a March 2017 talk entitled "Miyazakiworld: Popular Culture and the Uses of Enchantment," Professor Susan Napier of the Tufts University Japanese Program pointed out that Miyazaki's heroines often forgo the homecomings typical of heroes in Western narratives. It is almost as if once these heroines are in flux, they lose the ability to find their way home.

San stays in the woods, but her wolf-mother is dead; she has developed kinship with humans and can no longer return to the forest as an unequivocal home where she can willfully neglect the uncertainties presented by her body. We last see her with a wry smile on her face, far from the aggressive, wild girl we first met. Though Chihiro eventually wins her way out of the spirit world, we see her turn back at the end, her posture calm, measured, and mature—a far cry from the hunched, whining girl we met at the beginning of the film. The kernel she consumed changed her somehow: Perhaps she has just grown up, or perhaps she has left something of herself behind in the eerie spectral landscape—or perhaps she is a different girl entirely. Sophie, young again at the end of the movie but with her hair recently shorn, is last seen turning to kiss Howl on the deck of the moving castle. Her hair remains gray, a reminder of her time in elderly form, but her stance is confident and adoring. Self-doubt banished, she is radiant; though far from the home she originally set out from, Sophie is now at home in herself.

The films provide no neatly packaged conclusion for the continued ambiguities of their heroines' hybrid existences—girl or wolf? girl or spirit? girl or crone? The viewer and the heroines themselves might never know, and perhaps they aren't meant to. Perhaps, in never giving them the full-circle homecoming, Miyazaki is telling us something important about bodies in flux: There is no easy answer to be had; only the conflict, the question, and the transformation it offers. The reckoning of self happens in the space between the person one is and the person one is becoming. It is where we write our stories, where we recognize the complexity and turmoil of moving through this world in a body flawed and pressed upon by politics and expectation. Though they may not be the homes we started in, our bodies become the homes we inhabit.

Last month, I returned to Japan. After a haircut (just a trim this time), I descended the staircase into the subway, fed my green ticket into the wicket, and waited for a homebound train. A gust of wind churned through the tunnel, heralding the oncoming train. The familiar three-tone tune sounded and the doors of the train slid open. I stepped into the air-conditioned tube and heard the familiar hush that my half-foreign body in adulthood always seems to inspire—the uncomfortable sweep of glances to the floor, the shuffle of commuters to the edges of velvet-covered benches.

I walked to the suddenly clear center of one bench and sat down. I held my bag in my lap and looked straight ahead, catching my reflection in the dark subway glass. My familiar-alien eyes, my familiar-alien bones, my familiar-alien face, all looking back at me. I appraised myself: the new swing of my hair, the sudden unfurling of something like recognition, small but sure in my chest. I held my own gaze. I smiled.

How to Stop Saying Sorry When Things Aren't Your Fault

Kamna Muddagouni

A month ago, my mother told me she wanted to move back to India before she got too old. It wasn't the first time she'd raised the idea, but this time she seemed serious—like she was letting me know it will happen. My parents are the only family I have in Australia, apart from my partner. When pressed why, she said she and my father didn't want to have no one around when they were in their old age. It was as if she was saying having me was not enough. I knew that it wasn't my fault, I knew I was enough. I knew her feelings of loneliness were more about the remnants of a life of migration and distance than they were about me, or any way in which I'd failed to make her feel. But I looked at her and said I was sorry.

I have been trying to let go of saying sorry. I apologize to my parents, to my partner, to friends, to colleagues, and even to strangers. Most of the time, it's for things I cannot control, let alone be responsible for. From my manic searching on the internet, the habit of constantly saying sorry is not a trait of any diagnosable condition, nor a sign of any obvious sociopathic tendencies. But it is, from my personal experience, a problem.

My partner was diagnosed with a chronic illness two years ago. He has an autoimmune disease that has meant countless visits to the hospital, dragging periods of pain and discomfort, and a big shift in the way we live. He's had to adapt to pain, discomfort, and a changing body—daily reminders of an illness that may never get better. And I've had to adjust to my changing and uncertain role: to be partner and carer, to be lover and also comforter, all the while seeing someone I love so dearly suffer.

The doctors say there's no cause for his illness. It's just something that happened to him, through nothing he did and nothing he could have avoided. Yet, as each day passed, I couldn't help but say sorry to him. I apologized for when he felt unbearable pain. For his fatigue that meant days had to be spent in bed, and plans had to be canceled. When his friends stopped asking how he was, because the answer was always going to be a variation of not great, I said sorry to him. And when I was tired of carrying the weight of being the only one who was always there, I said sorry.

A while back, when I was in the middle of saying sorry for another day he spent in pain, he stopped me. "You know this is not your fault, don't you?"

I replied instantly, "Of course, it's just you're—"

He interrupted me, "I worry that when you try to make it easier for me by saying sorry, you're making it your fault that things are like this."

I dismissed the exchange at the time and quickly changed the topic. But I couldn't shake the feeling that what he said was true. I had become so caught up in apologizing for how hard things were that I had begun to think of myself as responsible for his discomfort and mine.

•

My parents, older sister, and I migrated to Melbourne when I was six. One day, in our sun-filled flat in Mumbai, my parents sat us down and said, "We're moving to Australia. It'll be good for your sister and you. It'll be a new start."

I can't remember us ever talking about what "good" would be or what they meant by a "new start." I liked my life in Mumbai. I had my family, my friends, and by a six-year-old's measure everything *was* "good." There are memories I have of Mumbai, of my father's late work nights, spending weekends away or at functions, and of my mother as the one who was around. I remember overheard conversations between my parents, of wanting better for themselves, their life, and their children.

I can't remember being privy to much more than that. All I understood about why we packed up our lives into four suitcases, and caught a flight across the world for a "new start," was my parents' belief that it would be good for me and my sister. While I can't recall my parents ever pointing the figurative finger at me, I felt the heavy weight of their decision to migrate.

It was the mid-1990s, on an unseasonably cold day in November, that we arrived in Melbourne on a public holiday called Melbourne Cup. The streets were dead and every shop we could see was closed. Our bright-eyed, brown faces tried to mask the growing feeling that maybe we had made a mistake.

Without any other family in our new city, the four of us clung to one another as we adjusted to our new lives. My parents tried hard each day to exude optimism. The supermarkets didn't stock any of the food my mother had used to make our daily meals in Mumbai. Yet in the absence of bhindi (okra), karela (bitter melon), and tindora (baby gourd), she fried French green beans and frozen peas with turmeric and chili powder, spices we'd carried with us in our suitcases to savor the taste of home. My father's high-ranking job in a government department in Mumbai didn't translate to the jobs in the newspaper classifieds, so he turned to his previously forgotten social work degree, determined to find a job, to support his family. My parents were trying to create a sense of home for my sister and me, masking the fact that they were worried about this decision they'd made for them and for us.

I had no language to explain to my parents that I knew how they felt, how I wished they didn't feel this way. I had no way of showing them I, too, was scared of the non-Indian faces at school who ignored me when picking teammates in their schoolyard games. Of the school teacher who made prejudiced assumptions about my English ability and mispronounced my name to the extent that it became something I didn't recognize as mine. I had no way of telling my parents, without compounding their own pain, that I could see beyond their enthusiasm to know they shared the same discomfort I felt.

So I did what I thought was right: I said sorry. I'd say sorry when we had to walk too far to carry our groceries home, even though it wasn't my fault we couldn't yet afford a car. I'd say sorry for the bad days at work where they were forced to repeat their perfect English in an Australian twang so their colleagues could grant them some level of acceptance. I'd say sorry when they couldn't resolve arguments they had because my mother felt they were repeating old patterns in a new country, where she was the one looking after the children as my father threw himself into his job. I'd also say sorry at school. I'd apologize to my teacher when I already knew the answers to the basic mathematical lessons he taught, because I had covered the same lessons in India. I'd say sorry to classmates because I couldn't yet understand the slang they uncompromisingly spoke to me.

When I look back at these instances in my childhood, I regret all the times I said sorry when it was not what I meant at all. I said sorry to fill in silences caused by feelings I could not convey to my parents. I said sorry because I felt the weight of their decision to leave our home, even though it wasn't my decision at all. And I said sorry as a way to mask my own feelings of shame for having to assimilate in a society that only saw me as different. As a child, unable to name and parse the complex traumas of diasporic life, I found meaning in apologizing. But in doing so, I lost the language to express my own discomfort and to give myself space to grieve.

While immigrating and caring for a loved one who has a chronic illness seem like two entirely different things, they both are processes in which I lost control and had to adapt to traumatic change. Unknowingly, I had carried apologizing, the crutch I had used as a child to survive migration, into adulthood. It was the crutch I was leaning on as I cared for my partner, rather than confronting my own sorrow.

•

"What's the word for 'sorry' in Hindi?" my partner asked me recently.

He started learning Hindi about five years ago. While there were gaps in his vocabulary built on some classes, apps, and very rudimentary "lessons" from me, "sorry" seemed like an essential expression he surely could not have missed.

"It's 'mujhe maaf keejiye,'" I replied to him, expecting him to respond with familiarity.

"That's 'please forgive me,' though," he said. "What if you're just saying 'sorry'?"

I stumbled back a reply. "I don't think there is a word for just 'sorry.' It's always about seeking forgiveness."

In Western culture, we're taught at an early age that the key tenets of good behavior fall somewhere between saying thank you and sorry. Say thank you when people do something nice for you. Say sorry when you've done something wrong, or when you've made a mistake, or when you might just have misunderstood. *Sorry* is a coverall. It's an accessible word to use when you can't always express what it is you're feeling beyond some amount of regret or sorrow.

The same has never been true for apologizing within my Indian family and community. "Sorry" is not an expression to cover the full ambit of situations that fill you with awkwardness, casual missteps, or pain felt by others. In its Hindi evocation, apologizing is a deliberate and conscious act accompanied by some form of personal reckoning.

When I left India, I was relatively fluent in Hindi. Though I never had the chance to properly learn it in a classroom, I have held it tightly. I feared that letting go of my ever-shrinking recollection of phrases would somehow mean letting go of my heritage and how I understood the world. Now the few occasions I get to speak in Hindi fall into the transactional interactions I have with my parents, my partner, and the "uncle" at the grocery store from whom I buy my aged basmati rice and imported frozen bhindi. I don't use Hindi to express my feelings, and so I hadn't used it to say I was sorry.

•

I have been trying to stop apologizing for things that are not my fault. When I think of all the situations when I would say "sorry" in English, to say "mujhe maaf keejiye" instead doesn't work. It doesn't work because it forces me to ask for forgiveness—something I cannot ask for or be given if I am not responsible for the hurt.

Thinking of apologizing in my home language has allowed me to understand the act of apologizing as inherently connected to asking for forgiveness. It reminds me that I do not need to blame myself for others' pain. I can empathize with it without the need to offer language to take personal responsibility.

By thinking of saying sorry in Hindi first, I pause my compulsion to say sorry and instead concentrate on what I could offer. I could offer love to my partner in his struggle with his illness. I could provide empathy to my parents for their ongoing difficulties caused by a life of migration and being part of a diaspora. And perhaps I could offer myself acceptance by refusing to apologize for myself in a Western world, by letting go of saying sorry for who I was and who I am.

In the spaces I occupy now, I think of how I can survive not by apologizing, but by using language as a way to articulate these feelings a younger version of me wasn't able to. I let go of saying sorry as a way of accepting what I can do and who I can be, and apologizing only in those moments when I truly seek forgiveness. Being myself is not one of them.

THE WAILING

Nadia Owusu

Downstairs it was hot and smelled like sweat, flowery perfume, and food—pepper soup, fish in palm nut oil, coconut rice. The fluorescent lighting added to the calming cold sterility of the guest bathroom where I hid from the wailing. In here, nothing had changed.

I managed to steal away by pretending I had a headache. I walked slowly up the stairs, leaving the ladies to continue their observance. They sat shoulder to shoulder, crammed into our small living room. Four of the eldest, most important ones were squeezed onto the couch; two large-bottomed ones perched daintily at the very edge of each of the two armchairs; the younger women squatted on the floor or on stools dragged in from the kitchen. Mrs. Karamagi, the loudest wailer, sat in my brother's tiny little red plastic chair, her hips spilling over the sides, her knees up by either ear as though to shield them from the sound of her own piercing cries.

Every morning for the past three days, they had arrived as the sun came up—a straight line of women snaking its way from the other side of the park. They wore colorful head wraps on which they balanced their trays of samosas, rice, and stew. I watched them from my bedroom window, marveling at this very common African scene playing out in this unlikeliest of settings: Rome in January. Men on their way for morning espresso stopped in their tracks to observe the exotic procession. Teenagers slowed their Vespas as they rode through the park, helmeted heads swiveling dangerously to get a better look.

The rules of civility required that the whole household be at the door to greet the ladies, to take the trays, to accept the ginger biscuits and condolences. But, as soon as I could, I escaped to the quiet coolness of the guest bathroom.

I hated the questions, the concerned looks. Most of all, I hated the wailing. I knew that the wailing was customary, that they were doing it out of kindness and tradition. Most of the ladies barely knew my father. In many African cultures, including the Ashanti tribe of Ghana, to which my father belonged, and the Chagga tribe of Tanzania, to which my stepmother belonged, it is believed that, after death, one is rewarded for living a good life by being made an ancestor. If a person is not properly mourned, it might be taken as a sign that he had not done enough to gain the love and respect of those around him. In this case, the dead person could become a ghost who will likely torment the living. There is no greater insult than to have your death ignored.

I decided that I would rather have my father around, even in the form of a troublesome ghost. And the theatricality of the mourning ceremony horrified me. I couldn't grieve because other people's flamboyant, feigned grief was all around me every second of the day. It was only when dusk descended that our guests wiped their faces with flowered handkerchiefs and, their voices hoarse, said goodbye until tomorrow. By then, I was too angry and frustrated to cry.

Once, he had been everywhere in this house, whether he was actually home or not. Even before the cancer, before he was constantly in and out of the hospital, he traveled a lot for work. When I missed him, I walked around poking through his things, rediscovering private jokes and familiar rituals. Every corner I turned, I could hear his voice, his gleeful laugh.

An old copy of *The Economist*, lying open on his desk in the study: "Nadia, come and read this article out loud to me. Let's hear what's happening in the world!"

Eggs and Nutella next to each other in the fridge: "Crêpes! Crêpes pour tout le monde aujourd'hui!"

Paul Simon's *Graceland* in the CD player: "*This is the story of how we begin to remember. This is the powerful pulsing of love in the vein.* Did you hear that line, Nadia? Did you hear it? He is a poet, Paul Simon, a true poet."

Soon his voice, the faint but steady whisper, was drowned out by the voices of the United Nations African Wives Association. To make matters worse, they had been cleaning nonstop as well. They picked up every old yellowing edition of the *Corriere della Sera* and the *Herald Tribune*; packed the legal pads covered in his scribbles into boxes; polished every surface, wiping away every remaining fingerprint. I was desperate to know that I could still find him if I needed him, but with them here, I couldn't poke through his things without attracting attention. And, with attention came more well-intentioned, but exasperating, cooing and coddling: Had I eaten? Was I all right? Did I want some tea with milk?

•

This last time, he had been in the hospital for a month. The ambulance came to take him away on a Saturday. The arrival of an ambulance was so much a part of our lives that no one woke me up to tell me. I stumbled down the stairs for breakfast as usual, half-blind without my glasses, wearing my fuzzy slippers and pajamas.

I was startled by an unfamiliar voice: "Buongiorno, signorina."

I squinted to make out two men carrying a stretcher, the thin body of my worn-out father lying on it.

"Baba?" I asked.

"Good morning," he said.

I couldn't be sure if he said it in reply to my question or if it was a reflex of deeply ingrained politeness. I couldn't tell if he knew that I was me and I didn't want him to go. The tumor in his brain had taken most of his memory.

"We're going to the hospital," said my stepmother, Anabel, emerging from the coat closet. "He had a difficult night," she added as she pulled on her hat.

Every night had been difficult—every night since they told

us that the cancer was too aggressive, his body too weak. Sometimes he was himself, just smaller and tired. Other times, all he did was stare blankly at the wall, talking to himself quietly in Twi, his native language that none of us, wife or children, could understand.

•

On the fourth day after he died, the women did not make their procession across the park. It was the day of the funeral at the American Episcopal Church on Via Nazionale. The house felt strangely still that morning. I had grown accustomed to the crowds, to slipping away from them. I dressed slowly: new black dress; black tights; soft black leather shoes that I had worn only once. I preferred my Doc Martens, but Anabel said absolutely not.

As I faced the drizzly day, it occurred to me that I had barely been outside all week. The day Baba died, I was summoned to the principal's office. My sister was already there, staring at the floor. A friend's mother had come to pick us up and drive us the hour from school on Via Cassia to our house on Via Laurentina. She offered no explanation, except that Anabel needed us to come home. Only when we stopped the car did she acknowledge why we were at home at lunchtime on a school day, telling us that we would get through it, no matter how impossible it might seem now. She didn't say what "it" was. She didn't have to. We stepped out of the car, through the front door, and right into the wailing, already in session.

The church was full. The ladies, wearing fancier versions of their procession dresses, were dispersed among the crowd. They were sitting with their husbands—my father's colleagues at the United Nations. Family and friends had flown in from Ghana, Tanzania, England, Germany, the United States, and Canada. I caught myself looking for my mother, hoping in spite of myself that she had changed her mind.

My mother left when I was two and I barely knew her. But she was my only living parent now—I needed her. Two days after my father died, I called her on the phone, my hands shaking. I didn't know what I feared until she told me that she couldn't come for the funeral. Arizona was too far from Rome. She had responsibilities to another husband, and other children. She left before I was old enough to grasp what the leaving meant. I had never been forced to face the rejection. Now here it was. I cut her off in the middle of her reasons and vowed that I would never speak to her again. I hung up on her and sat in the hard ebony chair by the phone, panting.

Closing my eyes, I held my breath until my heart stopped racing. I counted my losses and waited for the cold ice of them to melt into tears, but they hardened even more. They frosted and stuck to each other, heavy in my chest. The heaviness made me keep that vow to my mother for ten years, despite her attempts to reconcile. It made me slow to love people and quick to leave them, to hurt them before they could hurt me.

My sister and I took our seats in the front row, filing in after Anabel, who cradled my sleeping little half-brother in her arms. He had worn himself out from screaming bloody murder all the way to the church. He was six, and didn't understand why we couldn't stop at McDonald's.

The priest gave a sermon, the details of which I have no recollection. I was too busy thinking that this wasn't at all what Baba would have wanted. He was an atheist and attended church only when Anabel insisted, or when we were in Ghana and my grandmother threatened him. The last time that Baba and I had been in church together was for a friend's baby's baptism. The baby had projectile vomited over his mother's shoulder before he could be handed to the priest to receive his blessing. Baba had clapped his hands once, a giant smile on his face, before he realized what he was doing. He quickly corrected himself before anyone noticed his enjoyment, but whispered in my ear: "That baby's an independent thinker."

I imagined his ashes blowing in the breeze on his beloved beach in Accra. Instead, they would be placed in concrete at a nearby cemetery. Anabel said that we couldn't afford to make the journey to Ghana. I suspected that she didn't want to go there because she was engaged in a bitter fight with Baba's family. They had never gotten along. The night before the funeral, Anabel had accused Baba's sister of stealing a framed photograph of Baba from the coffee table. When my grandfather arrived from Ghana without a winter coat, Anabel refused to let him wear one of Baba's. She didn't want *them* taking anything out of the house.

Everyone argued over things they would later throw away. Dirty laundry was aired, and accusations were launched like grenades. They were all fighting over my sister and me. Baba's family wanted us to live with our aunts in England. Anabel said that, in his last coherent days, Baba had asked her to finish raising us. I was surprised that Anabel wanted us to stay with her. Our relationship had always been a roller coaster. When Baba got sick, we hit a steep dip and plummeted at high speed. At the moment, we were barely speaking, though when we did speak, there was a quality to her voice and a look in her eyes that spoke to a longing that I recognized—a longing for nothing else to change. We didn't know how to live without him. But, if we maintained the world exactly the way he built it, perhaps we could survive.

I had inherited Baba's atheism. Instead of God, Baba was my guiding force. I was afraid that I would never believe in anything again. I was afraid until Mrs. Karamagi began to sing.

Father Michael was introducing Baba's best friend, who was to deliver the eulogy, when the doors burst open. There stood Mrs. Karamagi. She paused in the doorway as everyone turned to see the source of the interruption. Regarding her audience seriously, she spontaneously began to sing a Swahili hymn, arms reaching for the sky. The only word that I could understand was "Mungu"—God. Her shrill voice filled the room. It sounded like a feral cat that had been splashed with cold water. People shifted in their seats, uncomfortably unsure of how they were to react to this impromptu performance. Just as she hit a note so high that I was certain the stained-glass windows would shatter, I caught my sister's eye. She smiled, I snorted, and we began to laugh, stifling our giggles in our hands, disguising them as weeping.

Necks craned in our direction. The ladies were eyeballing their fake-crying competition. I pretended to wipe away tears and was surprised to find real ones on my cheeks. Perhaps they were tears of sadness, perhaps of release. I didn't know what would become of me when I walked out of that church. This was the ceremony that marked the end of my life as I had always known it. But, in that moment, all that mattered was Mrs. Karamagi's horribly off-key song. Baba would have loved it. I could hear him laughing.

Writing Letters to Mao

Jennifer S. Cheng

The year my first book of poetry, *House A* (Omnidawn, 2016), was published was also the fiftieth anniversary of the beginning of the Cultural Revolution in China: a cleansing of oppositional ideas and artifacts that became a purging of books, art, relics, heirlooms, religions, words, and ultimately bodies. It was led by a man and myth, Mao Zedong, and it is no coincidence that my book begins with epistolary prose poems addressed to *Dear Mao.*

Once, a reader told me that my missives to Mao sounded like love letters, and because I was born to immigrants who fled a country that was shredding itself, I was appalled, disgusted, annoyed. But then I thought: A love letter is something broken, too. It cannot say what it longs to say, it circles around an occluded center, it tries to uncover a history between two points.

Writers always say that first books try to be everything: We want to imbue our inaugural words to the world with as much of ourselves, as deeply and comprehensively, as possible. When I first started writing letters to Mao in the summer of 2012, I didn't know where it was going. I wrote to him on days that were full of sun and a bright blue ocean outside my window. I wrote to him on days when the fog was so thick, the world appeared white and ghostly surrounding my apartment. I wrote about the ocean and the feeling of sleep: *slow-moving, blurry, immersive but obscured.* I wrote, *If sleep is an ocean, then it is because we are migrants inwardly sighing along to its many oscillations . . . awash in the knowledge of three: body, bodying, embodied.* I wrote about the cosmic trajectories of my parents moving around in my childhood house, about the fluidity of history and myth, about floods and tornadoes and how *my father stood watch at the living room window, looking for tunneling cones or roofs detaching.* I wrote about the migration patterns of birds, the texture of my mother's voice, the violence of bodies, the inheritance of tragedy, the angle of daylight through the curtains. I wrote, *Our home in the south of the island slept between the ocean on one side, and on the other large dark hills, so I could always know what it was to be at the same time cocooned and ready to arch a distance.* I wrote about home-building. I wrote about anger and I wrote about longing.

In these long blocks of lyrical prose, I was following an instinct I didn't fully comprehend. I felt each address open up a wide field that could contain all the disparate yet overlapping emotions, atmospheres, and histories I had been wanting to hold in one hand. It was like drawing a boundary around a grouping of stars or cupping some water from the sea. The blocks of text didn't try to parse the entanglements; they allowed the tension between sentences to carry all the absences, ambiguities, and silences I could never before say—how knowledge in an immigrant household so often comes in tides that approach and recede, how there are always gaps and missing ghosts, how all the fear and protection and silence and love comes so mixed together it would be a falsehood to separate them.

Dear Mao, I wrote, *If the world, drowsy, were to be washed in a sheen, perhaps we would all have some intuitive knowledge of the immigrant body.*

For me, growing up in Texas, Mao was in some ways like an estranged but unspeakable family member: a familiar face that looked more like mine than my classmates' at school; a name I knew but a body I had never met, like so many of my actual family members. There was no singular conversation but rather an evaporation of allusions: *Mao Zedong was the suffering of your family*, my mother might say as she dropped steamed pork balls into our bowls. *Mao Zedong was the loss of homeland's soul*, as she wiped the tabletop with a wet cloth. *Mao Zedong—*, she would say, in conjunction with a word that means *to harm, to wound, evil, calamity*. The sounds of his name uttered from my parents' lips carried a heaviness I didn't fully understand but accepted as the cosmology of my home. Less a person, he was more: fact, shadow, air. He was like a ghost woven into the lamplight, the threads of the carpet, the pattern the window blinds made on the floor in the late afternoon. To say I loved Mao would have been repugnant and inaccurate. But to say I hated him would have been inadequate in ways as well. What does it mean to experience a history of trauma and blood in ephemeralities, in residue?

My parents were children who were separated from their families during the Cultural Revolution in the midst of imprisonments, labor camps, and hasty escapes, so history for me was always something blurry, leaky, vague. There was so much I did not know, and even if I asked questions, I never received a straightforward or comprehensive answer. There were pieces here and there—bodies floating in the river, meals of porridge to stretch out food, lost family members—but all of this was interwoven with the rest of my childhood: the sound of my mother's bare feet on the linoleum, my father telling stories of the Monkey King each night with our stuffed animals, my brother and I chanting rhymes and songs in Mandarin and Shanghainese during breakfast at the table my father built. At some point I decided that either my parents didn't know much of their family narratives—a lineage misplaced among the turbulence—or they didn't have the language, linguistically or emotionally, to communicate with me about it. As for so many children of immigrants, their lives came to me in little fragments and echoes that I collected in my palm like rainwater.

Dear Mao, I hope you understand that what I am doing is trying to give you a history of water . . . History as water, so that I am giving you something that spreads.

Mao was loss: of family, of home. But in a strange, flawed way, he also came to stand in for the very thing that was lost: homeland. He was the catalyst for my life in America and therein for the cultural distance between my parents and me, but also, then, for the relative safety and stability of my life here, the ocean of love that my parents recovered in the space of that distance, the constellations and weather they spun inside the rooms of our home. How can I address this colossal specter of history as anything but all of my complicated feelings of anger, curiosity, tenderness, intimacy? What do I want from him when I say:

> It is important for you to understand that never once did I long for a different life, which is not to say I never longed for home . . . for although as a child I was often homesick—at school, at the neighbor's house, anywhere unfamiliar or foreign—I also at times felt an inexplicable longing while inside my own house.

Or:

> Some nights I dream of subtropical trees and their serpentine branches, but more and more my days are filled with escarpment and carapace scattered across .the beach. The shells are emptied, abandoned; they are waiting for history to declare them whole.

Despite their lack of explicit storytelling, my parents managed to hand down their own history lessons to my siblings and me, which were distinct from the history lessons I learned in school. I always knew who Mao was, just as I always knew to clean my plate, to save rubber bands and plastic bags, to sneak extra napkins at the cafeteria. Mao was a phantom, and like all phantoms, he was sometimes tepid and sometimes looming, appearing and disappearing in the cracks and crevices of our house as the loss and suffering of my ancestral homeland, the brokenness of my family, and sometimes in my child logic all that was sinful about the heart. *Dear Mao,* I wrote, *You were dust in my house. A shadow underneath the floorboards.* These lessons of Mao came mixed together with other ones: to be wary of strangers and unfamiliar situations; to keep to myself and carry out my work invisibly; that a home is something one leaves over and over. My parents' lives and histories, though unarticulated explicitly, have been internalized in the navigations of my body in the world, and in many ways, Mao became a name for so many unnameable apparitions.

Dear Mao, In stories we kept reading, wandering was a punishment, and we were instructed to pity the immigrant, the foreigner, the stranger. But what if the absence of a point of reference is not something to be lamented but a structural foundation on which to build a house we fill with water?

I often think about how some Chinese Americans have a more complex relationship to the history of China than the people who grew up or still live there, as if we are the black sheep of the family, the mislaid children who are always in some way measuring the distances surrounding us. There is a strange sense of estrangement in my body that leads me back to the ocean to count its waves. As I grew older I began learning that Mao, like my relationship to homeland and history, has a fluid and complicated shape. He is an abhorrent dictator to many and yet a revolutionary hero to others. There may have been beauty in his theories and ideals, but there were also bodies in turmoil and bloodstained hands. Fathers can be terrorizing figures as much as they are meant to be kind, so why should I not think of Mao as an odd manner of broken family member, a man and a myth, a perpetrator I would like to look in the eye, confront, rebuke, as well as a lost ghost to explain to, justify to—something to complicate and, yes, even to long for—an absence, a wound, to mourn?

All writers in some way compose love letters to their obsessions. A letter can be a document of deep ambivalences, contradictions, and silences, submerged in the complexities of shared and unshared histories. Or: a longing to locate two disparate points in an expanse of sky.

Dead-Guy Shirts and

Motel Kids

Niina Pollari

One afternoon in the 1990s, our friend Angie showed up at our house in Palm Beach Gardens wearing an oversized, second-hand polo shirt. Angie was closer to my sister's age than she was to mine, but when we were kids, we cohered as a group while our parents wasted the weekends away. Her tiny frame was swimming in the shirt, which to me looked chic—it was retro before I understood what retro was, the graceful claim of a style from outside your own time—and I was jealous of the effortlessness with which she wore it. Angie told us that the shirt came from a bagful of free clothes that used to belong to a dead guy. They were soft polos and button-down shirts worn almost to transparency, with his name written in marker across every tag: *Arthur B.*

My sister and I befriended Angie the way that kids make friends: by being around each other often enough. Angie's parents were the proprietors of the motel where my family landed after we arrived in Florida, and our fathers were acquainted with the same person—a glib, white-collar type whose business was helping newcomers "get established" by roping them into overpriced leases and dealings that would never turn a profit. Angie's family had been in Palm Beach County for years, operating the motel he hooked them up with, where we ended up living for our first few American weeks.

It's hard to explain that Florida wasn't strange to me at first. It didn't start being strange, in fact, until I left it behind and heard people from other states make it a punch line. In 1994, it was just a place where everything I could pick up and hold in my hands was new. My parents had visited, but only once, and they'd come back marveling in equal amounts about the EPCOT Center and about the existence of Happy Hour two-for-one specials. When they got back to Finland, they unloaded a suitcase of Costco candy and showed us pictures of themselves on rental bikes, leaning on palm trees, smiling in the sunshine. I went to school with a secret about how I wouldn't finish the year with my classmates.

Most of what was in those photos from their weeklong vacation wasn't particular to the state of Florida itself. They never saw any other part of the United States before deciding to move us there. Until I left it, I didn't know that in adopting Florida, I adopted all its freaks and swindlers and addicts and charismatic criminals too. Everything was new at first, and then when it wasn't new anymore, it was normal. This didn't happen in stages that moved from the grand to the particular, America first and Florida second. Florida was America.

To get there, we sold all our stuff and then took a meandering series of plane rides from Helsinki to Moscow, then from Moscow to Ireland, then from Ireland to Miami. The last leg of the flight took place on New Year's Eve on a bouncy Russian Airbus that served nine-year-old me sparkling wine as the clock struck midnight, St. Petersburg time. Upon our arrival, I threw up at the terminal; this is my first American memory. We remained stuck at immigration for hours. My sister and I napped agitatedly on the ground in between rows of seats as my parents tried to translate to the youthful officer what exactly we were doing in the country and why, sharing a single dictionary between them.

By the time the terminal finally spat us out, it was deep into the morning of January 1. I was delirious from the time difference, and the humid Miami air felt like breath on my skin, heavy and unreal. And then, a small miracle: We didn't expect anyone to be waiting, but there was Angie's dad, wearing a cowboy hat and holding a sign that said our last name. We piled into the car and he drove us north toward morning in his boxy old Cadillac the color of fool's gold.

•

I'd known we were to live our first days at the motel, and I'd packed into some nylon luggage everything we didn't sell or give away back home. But as my parents were flipping through their bright yellow book for the right words to explain the circumstances of our arrival, the airline, operating on a skeleton crew for the holiday, locked our bags away. Our things were supposed to follow us to Lake Worth later that week, but this also meant that we were in Florida with no clothes but the ones on our backs.

Back in Finland, I had a strict morning routine that consisted of eating thick-skinned oatmeal and then putting on my snowsuit and taking a long walk to school in polar semidarkness. I'd walk under a highway overpass and past a soccer field that, for most of the year, served as a hockey field. The field was always freshly plowed, and the snowbanks accumulated alongside it all winter, which, by the end of the season, felt like crossing a small mountain range to get to school. But at the Seven Palms Motel, there was no snow and no script to follow. It was hot outside, and my snowsuit had been sold. I wasn't enrolled in school yet, and I had no uniform to wear. So I flipped on the TV right in front of me and changed the channels until I found cartoons.

Later, my father returned from Kmart with a grab bag of clothes that included a bright neon swimsuit with vertical stripes. Pulling on the suit legitimized me into a motel kid, there on semipermanent holiday like the other kids of vacationers. I woke up, swam, ate whatever random fast food was put in front of me—Arby's, Burger King, Long John Silver's— and drained Pepsi after Pepsi from the mini fridge. The butt of the swimsuit pilled from my sitting on the pool's unpolished concrete rim before launching myself in. Winter was high tourist season, so there were lots of other kids, but they came and went, there for a week, two at most, and then they were gone.

But Angie and her older sister milled around every single day after school, like my sister and I, and eventually we all became friends. Angie's swimsuit was from Kmart too.

Eventually, my parents moved us from the motel into an apartment, got jobs, and enrolled me and my sister in school. But the vacation went on every weekend. The apartment complex was filled with other young Finns who liked partying on the weekends, some of them parents, some of them not. The centerpiece of the complex was the pool, so that's where everyone gathered to do vodka shots under the stars. I look back on it now and realize that my parents were just young adults who happened to have children. There were half a dozen of us kids; the pool was our domain during the daylight hours, and when the adults took it over at night, we roamed through the unlocked apartments doing whatever.

I recently watched Sean Baker's extraordinary *The Florida Project* and recognized so much of my childhood—we weren't mired in the kind of precarious poverty that the film depicts, but my parents made little money at the construction site and the nursing home, and so found their own small hustles to make ends meet. And though I wasn't nearly as unsupervised as the film's young protagonist, Moonee, I felt close to her when she chose to create chaos inside a system built by adults. I remember sitting undetected behind the shower curtain with my best friend at one of those parties as drunk adults used the bathroom. We froze into stillness every time someone entered, and stifled giggles every time we heard a fart. I still always look behind the curtain when I use strangers' toilets.

In pictures from that time, everyone looks so '90s Florida: florals and light denim and wraparound sunglasses on our sunburnt parents, bike shorts and Blossom hats on me and the other girls, the boys in swim trunks and oversized No Fear shirts. And hand-in-hand with the clothes is a memory of music, lingering across those weekend-long parties. I remember the accordion player with his big, gin-blossom nose; the way Angie's dad's lower lip stuck out as he hunched over his electric guitar; my own showboat father, shirtless in a vest and a cowboy hat, singing Finnish standards with his strong, warm voice. In the pictures, the blue-green light of the pool falls across everyone's faces as they're caught laughing into the morning hours. In the pictures, the hot wings never get cold.

Something I recognize now is that the parties often lasted long enough to turn a little weird, the way parties do if people don't want to move past them and into reality again. Someone made out with a person they weren't married to. Someone kicked out the window of a minivan. These people were our parents and neighbors, but at the time, they were just partying, the way I have found myself partying since. They were partying for their best selves, and to halt the time that was passing them by.

•

We'd moved to the north part of the county by the time Angie came around dressed in her dead-guy shirts. My father returned to Finland to nurse his deepening addictions, and my mother moved house to extricate herself from an immigrant enclave that started to feel stifling. My sister and I continued to live in hand-me-downs, secondhand trash dropped off at the house and rummaged through to create personal style. As I grew older and my body grew uncomfortable, I embraced oversized tees that I imagined hid things from the world. I was feeling around for an identity, and when Angie walked in wearing Arthur B, I saw one.

I remember the moment with the shirt so powerfully. The twinge of envy I felt was not about the object itself; it would never have looked right on me. What I was jealous of was the seeming deliberateness of the choice, and the nonchalance with which she wore it to the effect of personal style. It was just like how she and her sister were already at the motel, fully formed when we arrived and began our fumbling. To choose a way you want to define yourself and then dress deliberately toward fulfilling that vision was magic to me. It was a clean talent. I didn't know how to make other people see me, but I wanted to.

Angie and my sister continued to be friends, but my best friend moved back overseas, and I was lonely. Over time, my introversion steered me toward goth. As a style, it worked perfectly because it was aesthetically obvious in a way I liked: Visual signs that said *don't talk to me* were a way to have control over my friendlessness. Once I knew what I was going for, the task of browsing Goodwill racks and garbage bags of discarded club clothes was easy. When we went to the Goodwill, my sister gravitated toward grunge antifemininity, and I rifled through the racks for anything black or synthetic. Period details also helped—I wore ripped-up eyelet slips underneath every skirt and dress I had. My style, though uncomfortable in the heat, was finally beginning to feel like mine. It felt like a uniform, and after a while, it was even a way to make friends again: Say *Isn't it fucking hot?* to someone also suffering in vinyl pants in the sunshine, and you'll be guaranteed to have at least one thing in common. At least you're both committed.

In another picture I keep, I'm in high school, and it's taken on a night my new best friend and I are headed to the midnight showing of *The Rocky Horror Picture Show* in Lake Worth. We pose seriously in our regalia, our bangs gelled into spikes and our eyes lined all the way around. I have a studded dog collar around my neck. Next to us, there's my sister and Angie, wearing the discards from our goth dress-up pile just to amuse themselves. It's all vinyl and lace and feather boas, and they're making faces at the camera like they know it's corny and overwrought. I know it is, too, looking at the picture. But I didn't know it at the time, or didn't care, and now I feel tenderly toward my own seriousness—I look like someone who found something she was looking for and doesn't mind if other people notice.

At the end of *The Florida Project*, Sean Baker suddenly switches from a 35-millimeter camera to an iPhone to capture Moonee and her best friend as they run hand-in-hand into the happiest place on earth. It's a sudden change in perspective, too different from the rest of the film not to notice, and it has the effect of making you feel like you've left someplace. And, of course, you have. The film is often funny and charming because of its charismatic stars, and bleak equally as often because of its scenery and situations, and the ending scene feels like a fantastic diversion into unreality away from both of those things. There's no real-life equivalent of this sudden shift for me—maybe there isn't ever, for anyone. But something keeps me returning to these strange and golden moments, and when I look at the pictures that serve to corroborate the memories, I feel the blur of time, and I feel myself hurtling forward.

Mourning My Birthplace

Natalia Sylvester

The last time I was in my birth country, it was death that brought me. It was summer 2013, and my abuelito, my father's father, had spent weeks in and out of a hospital in Lima, Peru. He was in his early nineties, with a lifetime of survival from violence and health issues behind him, and so at first when his body began breaking down, it felt like another thing he would recover from.

My family in Lima and my father in Miami, who spoke to the fellow doctors in charge of his care daily, knew better. Their cycle of panic and hope and dread had slowly been exhausted; by the time my grandfather was rushed to the hospital in early June, a quiet knowing had spread over them all. Even from our hotel in Port Aransas, Texas, where my husband and I were celebrating our anniversary, I felt it. My father called just as we were sitting down to dinner next to a giant seawater aquarium. I watched the fish meander by as he told me it was time to say our goodbyes.

There is nothing that prepares you for the pain of mourning, but when you've spent your life apart from a loved one, what prepares you for not knowing how to mourn? My mom, my dad, my sister, and I moved to the United States from Lima when I was only four years old. While my childhood was spent with my grandparents, cousins, and aunts and uncles on my mom's side, my father's side of the family remained in Peru. We spent years unable to visit them while our immigration papers slowly made their way through the system. We got to know each other through charged-by-the-minute phone calls on birthdays and holidays, or vacations my grandparents took, bringing along a few of my cousins, to visit.

Which is to say, we didn't.

What few memories of my grandfather I can truly call my own, I've held on to like the faded photo albums my parents brought with them when they left Lima. There's an image of him going for a walk in the park with my father, a small, white towel hanging over his shoulders to wipe off his sweat. The sound of his laughter, so loud and deep it crackled. On one of his last trips to Miami, he petted our boxer, Chloe, with such gusto I can still see his hand slap against her wagging body. More than that, there is distance and silence.

In Spanish, to say "I miss you" we say "te extraño," or sometimes more fittingly, "me haces falta," which is to say, "I lack you." I lacked my grandfather and he lacked me, so when the time came to say goodbye, it seemed that leaving our country twenty-five years ago had already done the hardest work for us.

There is nothing easy about migration. It is a search for a better life, but in this way it is also a death. How easily would you choose to leave this life? How quickly, if the decision were made for you? It is a line you cannot uncross, whether you are lucky enough to visit every few years or if you left knowing you will never return. Everyone and everything you knew and loved are gone.

•

In the four days my father and I were in Lima, there was little more than half an hour of sun. Autumn was closing its doors to let winter in through the window and the sky was perpetually gray. Life became muted. Light slipped out of it. No one—not a single pedestrian, or stray dog, or even the towering half-done buildings that stretched toward the sky—cast a shadow upon the earth.

When we first saw Abuelito, my father explained what was happening to him in a calm, medical fashion. He pointed out the dryness of his eyes, the long seconds it took for the color to come back to his skin and nails when he pressed against them. I imagined this was how he coped, by explaining the inexplicable. I watched my grandfather and watched the life leave and wondered where it was going.

"Vamos," he would say, over and over. It was the only word that stood apart from so many others he tried to utter. "Let's go." He called my father's name sometimes. He squeezed my father's hand and opened his mouth when my father asked if he could hear him, but no sound came out. His silence struck me the hardest, because my grandfather had been an orator.

He was known for these booming, long speeches after Sunday dinners or over video chats with my father. He always had so much to say, and in those moments I found myself regretting I didn't do more to listen.

That first day, I wrote. *What I want for him now is peace and a chance to reclaim his words, if only for the last ones that are spoken.*

We had so little time with him that my father and I barely left Abuelito's side. Cousins, aunts, uncles, siblings, and friends of the family stopped by to pay their last respects, and we'd sit quietly in the background, or leave the room altogether.

On the second day my older cousin came in and sat at my grandfather's side. She took his hand, leaned into his ear, and began whispering. I tried to look away, or at least, tried to make myself look away. I did not want to hear what she was saying so much as I wanted to have as much to say. They spent minutes like this, with their heads pressed together. Every few seconds, Abuelito would nod, just barely, and I'd search myself for words to offer him: words that would take up as much time. Words that would make up for the time we never had. Words to say, I'll miss you. Words to say, I missed you. Meaningful words. Last words. Words I didn't have.

Our third day in Lima, my father took me for a walk through our old neighborhood. He took my hand and we crossed Avenida Benavides, a street now as thick and congested as a highway, though my mother recalls playing in its loneliness as a child. He showed me the building where we used to live. It had a bright yellow exterior and a thick strip of maroon blocks of brick underneath the windows. From the ground, my father pointed to the third-story window of our first apartment. It sat empty next to another unit covered by a huge "Se Vende" sign. We walked along the side of the building as a young woman rode up on her bicycle and entered. She lived there and we did not anymore.

"That was your room," my father said. "That's where you slept in your crib with your cast."

I nodded and remembered—not living there, but seeing a video of life there. It is a glimpse into a white-walled baby's room. My left leg is suspended in midair, covered in a cream-colored cast, after my first series of hip surgeries when I was one. My sister in the living room, having spilled a basketful of plastic barrettes, tries to chew on them like they're candy. After my parents' divorce in my mid-twenties I lost track of where this video went, but it is the closest thing I have to a memory of life in Peru.

On our last day, all four of my aunts and uncles arrived at the hospital, and for a brief twenty minutes or so, my grandfather was finally joined by all his children, together in one place. They told him, "Aquí estamos, Papá," because by then we did not know how much he saw or heard, and they wanted him to know they were all with him. He slept, and then he woke, and then, as if he'd been saving all his energy for this moment, he spoke.

"Lo que yo más quiero es hablar."

What I want more than anything is to speak.

We braced ourselves. We told him to go on. But that was either all he had to say, or all he could say.

His last words are a gift that has both haunted and consoled me. At times I think of them and am overcome by guilt: How do you make up for a lifetime of not listening? Other times I listen harder and realize he was also saying: *What I want more than anything is to be heard.*

These meanings are not two sides of the same coin. They are the life we could have lived together, and the ones we lived apart. They are a family carrying their same blood to separate lands. They are two ends of a phone call, coiled and stretched thousands of miles, longing to be close enough to whisper.

Should I Apply for Citizenship?

Bix Gabriel

We were late leaving the hotel. Lars, a friend and colleague, watched me cram my handbag with the last of the detritus I somehow collect when I travel: hand lotion, a pack of melted gum, stubs of boarding passes, key cards, earrings on the nightstand, a phone-charging cord, a stack of receipts that I'll never submit for reimbursement. Lars stored all his receipts in a small plastic sleeve; he was already packed, waiting. I grabbed the last of my belongings, and he laughed.

"Oh my god, Bix," he said, "what *is* that?" He pointed.

I became aware of the object I'd been clutching, so familiar to me it was an extension of my arm. It's maroon, leather, a rectangle with a small clasp that, when you release it, opens the case like a book. "This?" I asked, puzzled. "Why?"

Lars explained: It was worn out, the edges a dirty taupe where the leather had eroded, the clasp hanging off to one side like a limp limb, the case itself fat with age and numerous documents. It was out of place with the polished look I hoped my matching lemon-yellow-and-gray suitcase and handbag gave me, a sign of some kind of class legitimacy I aspire to while traveling. I shoved the case into my bag, shrugged. "It's just . . . my passport holder."

I had more important things to worry about. Lars and I were leaving Bangalore, India; he to travel more than a day back to Chile via Germany, and me to take the hour-long flight to Hyderabad, where I grew up, and my parents—no, my mother—lived. It was 2013, and I was returning to the city for the first time since my father's death three years before.

•

I fished out my green card from the same maroon case and handed it to the white immigration officer at a Customs and Border Protection counter at John F. Kennedy International Airport. I was returning from another trip to see my mother in India and I was anxious. It was July 2018, a month shy of my twentieth year living in the United States; a few days earlier, U.S. Citizenship and Immigration Services (USCIS) had announced that even permanent residents could be refused entry and/or deported.

But the gray-haired and jolly officer just said, "Ms. Gabriel, next time you come in, you'll be a citizen, yeah?"

Before I could reply, he grinned knowingly, and waved me on. For most everyone I know—in the United States and in India—there's only one answer to the question. But for many of us immigrants, the answer is more complicated than a straightforward yes.

•

In 1999, I took my first flight from Hyderabad to New York City. All I recall of that twenty-odd-hour journey are flashes: the blue upholstery of the airplane seat; the rough headrest on which I lay my forehead and wept the entire way; claustrophobia in the airport crowded with relatives before my flight; my father's trembling arm around me as I clung to him until I had to check in. I was twenty-two and couldn't wait to leave home. But at the airport it dawned on me: I was leaving my family, leaving my father. The last time he and I were separated for any extended duration, I was six, and raged with fever for days.

Earlier that day, my mother had tucked my ticket, passport, and two thousand dollars into a passport case. It was shiny and had the earthy, funky scent of real leather.

"Be careful," she warned, "pickpockets are everywhere." I laughed. "Well, this won't keep them away, Ma, it's practically an invitation!" Stamped in small gold letters on the front of the case was: PASSPORT.

I arrived in the States with the cluelessness of a twenty-two-year-old, two overstuffed suitcases of clothes I would soon stop wearing because they marked me as FOB, and the great advantage of the English language as my mother tongue. After two decades of being cosseted by my parents, siblings, and maids, I found myself broke in New York City, unable to cook even rice, and often complimented on my English.

Why did I come? The easy answer: education. I wanted to specialize in documentary filmmaking. In India, at the time, there was no further course than the master's I'd already completed. Another answer: All the years I'd lived in India, I never felt like I fit in. I was stifled by my city; I'd broken up with my first love; I was searching for . . . I didn't know.

•

I emptied out my passport case on an airline counter, this time in Dhaka, Bangladesh. It was 2014 and I couldn't find my green card; without it, the airline couldn't let me on the plane heading back to New York. The Bangladeshi man waited. I recalled my last act before I left on this trip weeks earlier. As a precaution—because I'm prone to misplacing things—I'd made a digital copy of the card. I saw it now, still lying flat on the scanner in Brooklyn.

I called my partner, then I called the airport in New York. I was panicked. Crying. Yet, somehow, confident that everything would work out. Perhaps because, despite his dismal record on deportations, Obama was president.

This was two years before Trump's election, before the constant, crushing fear and insecurity that is life now in the United States for many immigrants, as it is for Black, or lesbian or gay, or transgender, or poor, or . . . the list is endless.

Ultimately, that day, because of my partner's tenacity, his

charm, his whiteness, his native-born American citizenship, his maleness, and because I had digital proof of my residence, I was given permission to fly back to the States and pick up my green card at the immigration counter. I tucked it back into the maroon case, the same case I've traveled with and still do. It's practical. And familiar. Something known in unknown places.

•

My first few years in New York were a blur: wake up at seven, sleep on the subway, get to my first job, rush to the second one (babysitting, under the table), then the third (dog-walking, also cash, also illegal), attend classes in the evening, stay on for my fourth job at the school computer lab until one in the morning. I'd eat dollar hot dogs as a treat, shoot my thesis documentary on the weekends, sign up for a psychological assessment that paid fifty dollars and get diagnosed suicidal, hound the university for more scholarship money, get my first credit card, be both invisible and racially denigrated. I befriended other immigrants and women of color, fell in and out of love, leaned on my new girlfriends, fell out with white American friends after 9/11, financed the documentary on my Amex, submitted the film to festivals, won an award, and . . . my student visa expired. I had to choose: stay or return.

Why did I stay? I was almost $20,000 in debt, far more than I could pay back anytime soon, no matter what job I got in India. As the youngest, I could have turned to my older siblings; they would bail me out. I stayed silent. After all, I was an independent twenty-five-year-old woman! I had my pride. How could I go back penniless after living in America's streets paved with gold?

Besides, I was still searching.

In May 2003, I took the first job I found. No. I took a job I thought would make me happy. American optimism, meet immigrant reality. I gave up on documentary filmmaking because it was too expensive, but I was certain I could clear my debt. In my year of Optional Practical Training (OPT), which the U.S. government grants international students, I worked for an anti-domestic-violence nonprofit serving South Asian women. It was 2003; my salary, $26,000. In today's terms, that's about $34,000. Back then, my rent for one room was $500; in 2018, that same room rents at $1,200.

The truth is, I loved my job. I found a community of sorts: progressive South Asian women. Toward the end of my OPT, the organization applied for and obtained an H1-B visa on my behalf. I had three years to pay off my loans. I was broke.

In a coffee shop one morning, after three years at the job, I met with a couple of board members from the nonprofit. I'd written a letter of complaint to the board about the nonprofit's power dynamics, as well as its pay. I wanted fairness, more money, and for them to file for my permanent residency. The board members reminded me of my two promotions, that my salary was in the thirties now. And no, they couldn't sponsor me for my green card, not yet. They paid the bill as I cried into the oatmeal I'd ordered in the hope that eating would stave off tears.

•

Two things happened in 2006: I changed jobs; and I met a man—a white American, a New Yorker, an activist—at a panel on the role of men in ending violence against women. The man, his family, embraced me. He, *they*, helped me pay off the last of my debt.

A few years later, after enough salary raises, we sold his apartment and bought a home together. Then, days after the closing, on August 27, 2010—eleven years and three days after I first left India—my father passed away.

After the funeral, I felt I could never return to Hyderabad, my birthplace, and face his absence, present everywhere in the city synonymous with him.

When I first arrived in the United States, I established a ritual: No matter what else happened, I'd buy five-dollar phone cards and call my parents on Sundays. My mother would pick up the phone, we'd talk for fifteen minutes, she'd say, "Here, your father is waiting," and he and I would talk for about an hour, until the phone beeped—beeped—beeped and—

After his death, I switched to calling on Saturdays, unable to face the lacuna of his voice. Now I talk to my mother every other day, sometimes twice a day. Sometimes she remembers that we spoke in the morning, sometimes she remembers what we spoke about.

On a Friday in 2011, I stood in City Hall, with my brother, my best friend (another immigrant like me), and my partner and his family, for a ceremony that took less than three minutes. We were married; all I wanted was to go home and sleep away the anguish of my father's absence.

Within the year, my green card arrived. It had taken me twelve years, my father's death, and my subsequent marriage to become a permanent resident.

•

Now, in my twentieth year in the States, my father has been dead eight years. Three months ago, my mother, who still lives in Hyderabad, was diagnosed with an illness from which she will never recover. If I want to bring her here, I must become a citizen. But do I want to?

It's an enormous privilege to be able to consider this question at this time. Trump recently announced plans to send fifteen thousand U.S. Army troops to the southern border. Meanwhile, though I might feel out of place anywhere but New York, I can return to India; if I ever must leave the States, I don't have children I might be forced to leave behind and possibly never see again. I don't have a Muslim name, nor am I from one of the seven countries listed under Trump's travel ban. I am not Black nor Latina, I was not brought here without the required documents, nor did I fall out of status on a technical error like my best friend, who had to return to her home country after nineteen years. These are my privileges all.

Perhaps my greatest privilege is that I've been able to commit to my search—for myself, for what I craved and feared:

In 2014, I quit my job to pursue an MFA in creative writing, to write the stories I want.

This pursuit of passions—not for a better life or to avert poverty, nor to provide for family, nor, well, to live—underpins the American dream. What the dream narrative leaves out is that even embarking on its pursuit requires privileges. When Trump upholds immigration as a privilege, he is upholding privilege as a preexisting condition, and with it, the bedrock of privilege—its invisibility.

Every few phone calls, I ask my mother if she'll come to live with me in the United States. She never says no. Instead, she says things like: "You know I can't take the cold, even in the summer I use a blanket." "If you had kids, I would come right away. But now, what will I do?" "If I didn't have my school" (she's been running a school for underprivileged children for twenty-five years) "I'd go absolutely bonkers."

•

The day after Trump's election in 2016, I drove a friend, an Indian woman visiting me in Indiana, to a "quaint" touristy town nearby. I was conscious of leaving the progressive college-town bubble I lived in, of us being brown among a majority of whites, of Indiana being a red state. I say "conscious of." I mean, "terrified."

Now I'm more numb than afraid. Have I become inured to the constant attacks? Or does my privilege protect me from the impact of Trump's policies? I know what's real as a wound to me: my mother's health, my mortgage, the fear that without citizenship, I might lose the people I love, the place I call home, my personhood.

Is it as simple as taking a test, making a pledge, replacing my dark blue Indian passport with another dark blue passport, wedging it into the maroon case as if it's always been there?

My immigration has been one of choice, self-determination, of debt, and of privilege. Yet before I fill out the application for citizenship, fear reveals what is as invisible as privilege: that there is a point where self-determination confronts power and authority. Ask anyone who applies for a credit card, or a home loan, or a job. Ask most poor and/or Black or immigrant folk. Exercising your choice doesn't always result in getting what you want. This is the unspoken fallacy that determines who lives the American dream, and who doesn't.

Sometimes I wish for an uncontrollable outside event, the hand of God, to choose for me. Sometimes I want to ask strangers, like you, to decide: Should I—an immigrant to, a writer in, and a critic of the United States—apply for citizenship?

How to Write
Iranian America;
Or, The Last Essay

Porochista Khakpour

1.

Begin by writing about anything else. Go to the public library
in your Los Angeles suburb and ask for *all the great books people
in New York City read, please.* Wonder if the reference librarian
knows a living writer and ask her what would a living writer
read—*and an American one, please.* When she realizes you are
still in single digits and asks, *Where are your parents, young lady?*
don't answer and demand Shakespeare and take that big book
home and cry because you can't understand it. Tomorrow, go
back to reading the dictionary a letter at a time and cry because
you can't learn the words. (Ask your father if you will cry daily
for the rest of your life, and remember his answer decades later:

When you are older you will care less about things.) Pray to a god you still believe in that you will once more avoid ESL with all its teachers who look to you with the shine of love but the stench of pity: *refugee, resident alien, political asylum, immigrant, foreigner* the only words you know that you don't want to know.

Write because it's something to do, something your parents will let you do because it looks like homework. Write because one place to live is in your head and it's not broken yet; write because it's something to drown out the sound of their fighting deep into every night. When the second-grade teacher—the teacher your father calls an alcoholic—tells you that you will be an author one day and suggests *The Market Guide for Young Writers*, step right up and call yourself a Young Writer. Decide to really write and write about anything but Iranian America. *Ghosts. Victorian girls, maybe ones with tough names. Easter bunnies that are homicidal* (you might have ripped off *Bunnicula*). *Candy. White girls. More white girls.* (Even then you understood sales.) Worry about the fact that your family won't be able to afford a computer and worry about how your fingers get stuck in between the keys of a yellow typewriter your father brought back from Iran, and learn that the only way for your brain not to spiral in worry is to write.

Worry about how you, Young Writer, will ever get to New York City, until you do. Get a scholarship to a fancy college with writers and *writing workshops*, a thing you've heard of, full of other students told they'd be an author one day. Ignore the dorm politics and the suitemates who tell you their dads paid for you to be there, and write, write about anything else. *Los Angeles. The devil. Literary theory. Art. The East Village. White men. And more white men.* Become known as a writer there, a writer who doesn't write about that, in a time when everyone is talking identity. No identity for you, you tell yourself, you tell them. Wear black and smoke cigarettes and big glasses, because you are a New York Young Writer, and that can be anyone. When your favorite professor in senior year fails your paper on Modernism that you've worked on for weeks, when she tells you that she can tell English is your second language, when she tells you maybe writing is not for you, that maybe you need to go into a field like those new *Iranian Studies fields*—you keep imagining these *fields* like those villages of your homeland they label "third world"—go to your dorm and expect to cry but don't. Chain-smoke a pack of cigarettes and never forget her words and commit yourself to writing more, writing more about anything else.

Years later, attend another prestigious college for grad school, and spend long hours with a famous writer as your professor and adviser who tells you to forget that other professor, that you are a writer, that you can do this. Hold on to her words and almost miss it when she says, *but why don't you write what you know?* Thank her as you always do and hope she doesn't see your tears—*writing what I know was never my thing*, you whisper. Keep turning in stories about anything else. *Math. Chaos theory. Rape.* (The time you were raped but in a sci-fi premise; the time you were raped in a fantasy premise; the time you were raped in something they call metafiction.) *Dogs. Suicidal people. Suicidal people with dogs.* And *9/11*, which gets a little too close to writing what you know, but keep reminding them it was because you were a New Yorker, not because you were a Middle Easterner, that you felt the trauma; keep reminding them the hijackers were not Iranian. When they tell you they don't know what you are anyway, don't say a word, just keep working harder than they ever will and tell yourself you will beat the ones who hurt you most for that fellowship for another year. Get the fellowship and avoid all their eyes.

When your adviser suggests you work on a novel—that you are, after all, a novelist—hear *novel* like a curse: an arranged marriage and a death sentence, all that unknown potential for devotion to writing anything else.

2.

Until suddenly you can't write about anything else. Sit in your first apartment without a roommate and realize you have nothing else to write about for the span of a novel. Hate yourself and it, and then go ahead and write it, your Iranian America, because no one else will see it. This is your first real novel and what do you know. You are a fellow at the most famous university in Baltimore, which doesn't pay you enough to teach, so you add on being a hostess at a bistro where the parents of your students go, sometimes with the tenured professors of your department who pretend they don't see you as they kiss and hug the owner who sexually harasses you every day. Why would a word you write matter?

Quit smoking, start smoking, quit again, start again.

And watch it come out, more and more in every draft: anger with your parents, frustration with your blood, anxieties surrounding the somehow still-new land—all that is Iranian America. Let your truth come out hard and fast and untranslatable because no one else will see it anyway.

3.

Until they do. Four years later, after all sorts of troubles, it is your first novel and it is published and you are *Miss Literary Iranian America*, a friend jokes. *First Iranian American novelist*, a journalist mistakenly writes, while another calls your debut novel the first work that is entirely Iranian American, all diaspora with no Iran setting, which gets closer to the truth but you want to think still not close enough. Who can even tally who they ignored before you? When they ask you to represent the Iranian diaspora in Los Angeles, start by explaining you grew up a half hour and many realities away from Tehrangeles, that your family could never afford those areas, that you were raised in a tiny apartment in the low-income district of a small suburb, with no Iranian people.

When they ask you to do it anyway, go through with it. Regret quitting smoking. Try to speak of other things. *But about Iranian Americans*, they always go, and a friend who is tired of your sighs tells you, *Look, you did that to yourself, it's all in your novel.* Say *fair enough* and start smoking again.

Around Persian New Year, months after your first novel comes out, start to run out of money again. Old problem but maybe now a new solution, you think. Ask friends if they know someone at the most respected newspaper of the country—the venerable paper where they gave you a very good review of your debut novel. Pitch a piece on Iranians celebrating Persian New Year that 2008. Your angle: being Iranian in a bad time to be Iranian. Think to yourself, when was there ever a good time to be Iranian here, and pitch it anyway. Hear nothing back and tell yourself you and your Iranian America are not yet worthy of that newspaper.

Be more shocked than gracious a few months later when, out of nowhere, an editor at another section of that very paper writes to you and mentions he is a fan of your work and would you like to contribute an essay to this author series on summer? You can't believe it—this editor has acknowledged your novel and yet is not asking you to write a particular thing about Iranian America. But when you sit down to write, surprise yourself: It's about your mother and you, and so it's about Iranian America. Feel slightly defeated—*writing what I know was never my thing*, you know you used to whisper—but a part of you anticipates they will want this, and they do.

Behold the awe of everyone around you, behold your own awe: You are in your dream paper, an essayist suddenly. Editors who never heard of you or your novel start asking for your essays of Iranian America. Soon you are back in that same paper with another essay, about, of all things, Barbie's fiftieth anniversary and somehow you make it also about Iranian America.

You've learned to interview your parents and dig up whatever they will give you from their past and add that to messy memories of your childhood and glue it all together: an essay on Iranian America! Be amazed at how your formula sometimes helps you work out some things, be amazed at how it sometimes seems to help others. Remind yourself this can't last. Iranian Americans from all over the country write to you and thank you, and you tell everyone this was a nice run—you did your part—and now you will go back to what you were meant to write: anything else.

4.

Except you don't. They ask and you keep writing it. Tell yourself this is your new life every time an essay comes out in that venerable paper of yours—you start to call it *yours*, because three-figure checks must mean love if two-figure checks mean like, or so you tell yourself. Occasionally try to remind them you were a journalist before all this, a writer who wrote about music and art and fashion and books, but no one remembers or cares anymore. Editors start asking for a collection of essays, but you think, I've just begun. Tell them in 2009 you're just entering your thirties, what do you know?

Know you're an essayist and know you can't back out now. During an interview someone asks you why essays, and you remind them you write fiction and they ask again why essays, and you joke about them finding you, and they ask again why essays, and you stumble on another answer: *service*. That somehow your people are not visible, these three decades of being in the United States, and people have needed you and while you can't speak for everyone, you can speak some part of this truth. *Service? Service.* Afterward, bum the few cigarettes the interviewer offers and smoke through a silence you did your best to create.

Start to wish other Iranian Americans would write essays; even try to introduce to editors the few who seem interested, but the editors always ask for more essays from you. How many essays can you write, you wonder, but every time one comes out you start to see how they see it, and you see more. Step back from yourself and spin absolutely everything from the lens of Iranian Americana. An Iranian American sensibility, an Iranian American outfit, an Iranian American state of mind, Iranian American flora and fauna, an Iranian American bowl of goddamn fruit. Watch yourself pitch the editor at the venerable publication an essay on the hit TV show *Thirtysomething*, a show you loved, and because in 2009 it's a big deal that it's out on DVD and it seems like something to watch it in your thirties now. Hear the editor in your head long before your real editor asks you if you can include your Iranian American family in it, and catch yourself saying *yes, of course*, and do it, and never imagine years later you will teach that own essay of yours as a mistake. Consider later that maybe you knew and didn't care, you knew the *service* and moreover you knew your function: You were not just writing Iranian America, maybe you were helping them create it.

Write the Persian New Year piece you once wanted though it's no reported piece, but a personal essay—that's what they want and that's what you deliver. By this point your parents know why you are asking when you call, by this point they have gotten used to the fact that you will write about them and anything else Iranian America. When friends and family begin to marvel at all this, Miss Literary Iranian America, don't you deny it—smile and be grateful and lie that this is exactly what you dreamed of one day.

When another section editor of that same paper emails you (a section that pays a lot more—if three is love, four figures must mean marriage), accept their request for a new essay, knowing that you can write an essay on absolutely anything for these people, provided it's about Iranian America—which it will be. Muslim reality TV the first time, Iranian reality TV the second time, *but we're big fans of your essays, so can you make it an essay not a review?* They want feelings, not facts, you know this by now. Write the first and write the second and duck all the love hurtling itself at you, a love you can't feel, a love you might fear.

Writing Iranian America turns out to have some downsides, but you think you know how to handle them. When Iranians write to you and say you are not Iranian enough for them, thank them, and when others say you are too Iranian for them, thank them, too. Too pro-Republic and too Royalist, too anti-Iranian and too nationalistic, too relatable and not relatable enough, maybe neocon and maybe communist—and where is your name from? Are you really Iranian? Why are you not married? Are both your parents really Iranian? Why do you say Iranian and not Persian? Why are you embarrassing us? Why are you not writing happy things? Why are there so many jokes? What do you think of us? Are we good or bad? Are you good or bad? Why do you call us brown? Why are we not brown to them? Why do you not look more white? Why do you look so white? What god is your god? Why can't you write in a way I can understand? Why do you write at all? Why don't you stop writing? Why don't you stop smoking? When you get those messages, learn to let them say what they need to say. Occasionally engage, and often don't. *Service.*

Learn to live with hating yourself. Learn to live with hating Iranian America. Imagine the hell of dying in America while your parents envision the beauty of dying in Iran, and you wonder if there was ever anything in between for you.

5.

When your editors leave the section where they first published you and when the paper experiences horrible layoffs, think, this is it, what you've been waiting for—your run is over. Tell everyone you know it's been great, four years as an essayist of Iranian America! Imagine all the topics you were supposed to write about but you can't quite remember what. Try to remember and fail. *Hip-hop? White girls? Bars? Wars?* Try to remember and fail.

When a few years later, new editors are back in that old

first section of that venerable paper that made you Young Essayist, pause at the first line of their email to you. A pitch in the greeting, a story you know of: An Iranian band in Brooklyn has been the victim of a murder-suicide. For days you've considered reporting on this, thinking of the right venue, but now here is the op-ed section again wanting a personal essay. "It seems to me like there might be something interesting to say, about the Iranian expat community, the American dream betrayed, or something along those lines." Think about her take for a moment and think about how you can't: how this story has nothing to do with assimilation but is about a deranged person from your part of the world who shot some people from your part of the world, and is much more about gun control and America and its dream not betrayed at all. Ask her if you can face America here, not just Iranian America, in the only piece you can write, pitch this to her and know the answer.

Remind yourself that you have been chronically ill for many years and buying cigarettes is no longer an option.

Write for other sections of that paper—the book review, where you sometimes wonder why they don't give you topics relating to Iranian America—until once again, in 2017, another editor from that section writes to you, this time with a name that is definitely of Iranian America. When she says she wants a Persian New Year piece, a sweet nostalgia piece, remind her that four years ago, many editors ago, you wrote one. Tell her you have nothing happy to write this year and you weren't going to write this, and tell her your idea of New Year in the time of the Trump administration's Muslim ban.

Remember your first Persian New Year pitch to this paper, being Iranian in a bad time to be Iranian, and now a decade later witness that same silence with awe. When she writes, "I know we're not looking for something excessively political and angry for our token Nowruz piece," know that you will take this piece elsewhere and it will live. Try to put away any disappointment you have for her, your fellow Iranian American, because ultimately both you and her are microscopic cogs in the venerable paper's unfathomable machinery. Both you and her have come this far, both you and she might never know exactly why.

Observe others writing about Iranian America. Encourage and amplify the many voices and viewpoints of your people, now nearly four decades a minority in this America, finally with their own stories surfacing too. Enjoy reading their accounts, until readers warn you against your own enthusiasm. *I feel like they're ripping you off,* go messages from the concerned, and you don't know what to make of it. Against your better judgment, read more closely. Decide you will pretend not to notice. Pretend you are better than this competitive game they have set up for all of you to destroy yourselves in. Pretend so hard that you wonder if you ever even knew how that game works to play it anyway.

Pretend to chain-smoke a couple packs of cigarettes, killing hours in bottomless depression—pretend you're all smoke and ashes, let it burn right through you—and pretend Iranian America is all theirs, whoever wants this wreckage.

6.

Tell yourself this is the Last Essay, but remind yourself of all the other Last Essays. Wonder how much more of this you can take. Count that out of seventy pieces of nonfiction you've written since your first book came out in 2007, forty-eight have had to do with Iranian America. Ask yourself if it's too much or too little given where America is at, still at. Watch the news and marvel at how your entire life they obsessed over your country of origin, and continue to. Wonder if you and your family will end up in Muslim Camp after all. When people look at you with the pity and the regret again—*refugee, resident alien, political asylum, immigrant, foreigner*—let them have it, and let yourself take it. What has changed but nothing at all?

Write about it and make sure you keep writing about it. Plan out three more books and call it the end; each and every one is about Iranian America. Write all the secrets like every essay is a suicide note: one that reveals your Zoroastrian name is a fraud and you are a Muslim and watch everyone applaud it, from all sorts of people online to your own father, who gave you your name. Wonder if anyone is reading properly. Put "Iranian American refugee" in your Twitter profile, the way all the other refugees are doing. Question if this is empowering. Imagine you've been throwing yourself off a cliff every time you've been writing, but it's hard to know if you are killing yourself or trying to fly. Wonder if a cliché like that is all you've got. Wonder if the death you've been imagining is just you becoming a bad writer.

Watch yourself making posts on Facebook and Twitter more than ever in 2017. Watch Americans at first dive into it and then over time walk away from it, until you start to find yourself asking white people to repost or echo the same sentiment, so your ideas can get heard. Watch white Americans listen to one another but suddenly they are not so sure about your words. Remind them that you know Iranian America and that they seemed to love reading you—quote your own pieces, send them the links, remind them they knew you—but watch them slowly back away. Watch other friends tell you that you are reading into this, it's not happening. Watch yourself worry about every word. Watch yourself apologize for things no one understands. Watch yourself think only in Farsi, like this— America—never happened. Watch yourself burn out on the worry and remind yourself of where this essay started: Begin by writing about anything else. *End by thinking about anything yourself,* you tell yourself, but look at how you're all out of jokes about smoking.

7.

Be a little astonished that there is still one more section of the Last Essay, which is not the Last Essay, you and your editor and whoever is still here must know by now. Notice you've learned a few things about essays in this decade, and the ones you must write will write themselves for you. Remind yourself that when the performance is honest two things happen: The essay will feel like it's killing you and the ending will not be what you thought it might be. Learn to respect more than resent those parallel planes of living and the rendering of living.

Note that you're not thinking about this when you read and then reread an email you receive late one night a few weeks after this first Persian New Year of the Trump administration, from an Iranian American aspiring writer who tells you your work has saved her life, a woman twenty years your junior who asks if you have any words of advice. You thank her and feel embarrassed for your discomfort in reading her praise, and you try to channel her joy and enthusiasm and you fail, and you draft an email where you tell her to run but don't say which way. *One word: Run. Run with everything you've got, dear reader.*

Delete the email and start over, and watch weeks and weeks go by. One day open the draft and see the word *love*. Try to delete it but it won't go away. Tell yourself your delete key is broken and get it fixed and still try. *Love.* Tell yourself it was sent to you for a reason—laugh at the audacity, the idiocy, the cliché—and one day, many years into a version of a future you might get, go as far as to grow into it again.

Thank you, the young woman writes. *I think I know what to do.*

You wait for more, but that's it.

Acknowledgments

Thank you to every author in this collection; to Yuka Igarashi, founding editor in chief of *Catapult* magazine; to Catapult publisher Andy Hunter, editor in chief Jonathan Lee, and associate publisher Jennifer Abel Kovitz; to Matt Ortile, Megha Majumdar, Mallory Soto, Morgan Jerkins, Allie Wuest, Leah Johnson, Allisen Hae Ji Lichtenstein, and all our *Catapult* magazine colleagues past and present; to Nicole Caputo, art director for Catapult and cover designer for this anthology; to all the writers who have trusted *Catapult* with their work; and to our families for their steadfast love and support.

About the Contributors

LAUREN ALWAN was born in New York City and raised in Southern California. Her fiction and essays have appeared in *The O. Henry Prize Stories*, *The Southern Review*, *Bellevue Literary Review*, *StoryQuarterly*, *Catapult*, *Alaska Quarterly Review*, *ZYZZYVA*, and Nimrod's *Voices of the Middle East and North Africa*, among other publications. Her work has received the Goldenberg Prize for Fiction and been cited as Notable in *The Best American Essays*. She is a prose editor at *the museum of americana: an online literary review*. She lives in Northern California.

CINELLE BARNES is a memoirist, essayist, and educator from Manila, Philippines, and is the author of *Monsoon Mansion: A Memoir* (Little A, 2018) and *Malaya: Essays on Freedom* (Little A, 2019), and the editor of a forthcoming anthology of essays about the American South (Hub City Press, 2020). She earned an MFA in creative nonfiction from Converse College. Her writing has appeared in *Buzzfeed Reader*, *Catapult*, *Literary Hub*, *Hyphen*, *Panorama: A Journal of Intelligent Travel*, and *South 85*, among other publications. Her work has received support from VONA, Kundiman, the John and Susan Bennett

Memorial Arts Fund, and the Lowcountry Quarterly Arts Grant. Her debut memoir was listed as a Best Nonfiction Book of 2018 by Bustle and nominated for the 2018 Reading Women Nonfiction Award. She was the 2018–2019 writer-in-residence at the Halsey Institute of Contemporary Art in Charleston, South Carolina, where she and her family live.

VICTORIA BLANCO is a writer from El Paso and Ciudad Juárez. She received her MFA in creative writing from the University of Minnesota, where she taught creative writing and composition courses. Her manuscript was a finalist for the 2016 PEN/FUSION Emerging Writers' Prize. Her research and writing have been supported by a Fulbright Award, research fellowships from the University of Minnesota, the Minnesota State Arts Board grant, a Bakeless Scholarship from Bread Loaf Orion, a writing residency at St. Paul's East Side Freedom Library from Coffee House Press In-the-Stacks, and the 2018 Roxane Gay Fellowship in Creative Nonfiction for the Jack Jones Literary Arts writers' retreat. She was a Fellow in the 2017–2018 Loft Mentor Series. Victoria's writing has appeared in *Catapult*, *Fourth Genre*, and *Bat City Review*.

JENNIFER S. CHENG is a poet and essayist. Her second book, *MOON: Letters, Maps, Poems*, was selected by Bhanu Kapil for the Tarpaulin Sky Book Award and named a *Publishers Weekly* Best Book of 2018. She is also the author of *House A*, selected by Claudia Rankine for the Omnidawn Poetry Book Prize, and *Invocation: An Essay*, an image-text chapbook published by New Michigan Press. She is a National Endowment for the Arts Fellow, and has received fellowships and awards from Brown University, the University of Iowa, San Francisco State University, the U.S. Fulbright program, Kundiman, Bread Loaf, and the Academy of American Poets. Having grown up in Texas, Connecticut, and Hong Kong, she lives in San Francisco. www.jenniferscheng.com.

NINA LI COOMES is a Japanese and American writer from Nagoya, Japan, and Chicago, Illinois. Her writing has appeared in *The Atlantic, Catapult,* and *The Indiana Review.* You can read more of her work at www.ninalicoomes.com.

BIX GABRIEL is a writer, teacher, fiction editor at *The Offing,* co-founder of TakeTwo Services, occasional Tweeter, and seeker of the perfect jalebi. She has an MFA in fiction from Indiana University, and is completing a novel involving the war on terror and Bangladesh's 1971 war for independence, set in New York City, Dhaka, and Guantánamo Bay. Her work has appeared or is forthcoming in *War, Literature & the Arts, Longleaf Review, Catapult, Guernica,* and *Electric Literature,* among other publications.

NUR NASREEN IBRAHIM is a television producer by day and a writer in all the hours remaining. Born and raised in Pakistan, she is currently based in the United States. She has been twice nominated for the Salam Award for Imaginative Fiction. She has written essays and reviews for *Catapult, The Millions, The*

Collapsar, Barrelhouse, Dawn, and other publications. Her fiction has appeared or is forthcoming in *Specter Magazine, Platypus Press*'s digital shorts series, *Salmagundi, The Aleph Review, Barrelhouse*, and *The Gollancz Book of South Asian Science Fiction* from Hachette India.

DEEPTI KAPOOR is an Indian writer currently based in Lisbon. She gained Portuguese residency with the specter of Brexit looming, but lost her cat to the jungle on the way.

POROCHISTA KHAKPOUR is the author of *SICK: A Memoir*, named a Best Book of 2018 by multiple outlets, including *The Paris Review, GQ*, and *Time*. Her debut novel, *Sons and Other Flammable Objects*, was a *New York Times* Editor's Choice, one of *Chicago Tribune*'s Fall's Best, and the 2007 California Book Award winner in the First Fiction category. Her second novel, *The Last Illusion*, was a 2014 Best Book of the Year according to NPR, *Kirkus Reviews, BuzzFeed, PopMatters, Electric Literature*, and many more. Among her many fellowships is a National Endowment for the Arts award. Her nonfiction has appeared in *The New York Times, Los Angeles Times, Elle, Slate, Salon*, and *Bookforum*, among other publications. Born in Tehran and raised in the Los Angeles area, she now calls New York City her home.

SHING YIN KHOR is a cartoonist and installation artist exploring collections, memory, immigrant identity, and new human rituals. They founded the immersive installation art group Three Eyed Rat, which has built large-scale space desert apothecaries, decrepit space salvage stations in the forest, and lumberjack-themed bars.

SORAYA MEMBRENO is a daughter of Nicaraguan immigrants and a pre-LeBron Miami native. A poet and essayist, her writing has appeared in *Bitch*, *Catapult*, *Post No Ills*, and *The Racial Imaginary: Writers on Race in the Life of the Mind*. She is a member of the Online News Association's 2019 Women's Leadership Accelerator and has worked in fund-raising and development for various literary nonprofits, including *Poets & Writers* and Cave Canem. She currently serves as the director of community at Bitch Media, where she obsesses over funding models and the future of independent feminist media. She lives in Los Angeles, where she is hiding from winter indefinitely.

KAMNA MUDDAGOUNI is an anti-discrimination lawyer, writer, and campaigner based on the stolen lands of the people of the Kulin Nation. Kamna's writing practice explores intersections between feminism, pop culture, and political identity, her experiences as a third-culture kid, and legal rights for young and marginalized people.

JAMILA OSMAN is a Somali poet and essayist from Portland, Oregon. A public school teacher for many years, she is now an MFA student at the University of Iowa. A VONA/Voices alumna, she has received fellowships from Caldera, Djerassi, and the MacDowell Colony. She was cowinner of the 2019

Brunel International African Poetry Prize, and the 2019 winner of *The Adirondack Review*'s 46er Prize for Poetry. Some of her work can be found in *The New York Times*, *Al Jazeera*, *BOAAT*, *Diagram*, and other places. She is currently working on a memoir.

NADIA OWUSU is a Brooklyn-based writer and urban planner. Simon & Schuster will publish her first book, *Aftershocks*, in 2020. Her lyric essay chapbook, *So Devilish a Fire*, is a winner of the *The Atlas Review* chapbook contest and was published in 2018. Her writing has appeared or is forthcoming in *The New York Times*, *The Literary Review*, *Electric Literature*, *Catapult*, and other publications. She is the recipient of a 2019 Whiting Award. Owusu grew up in Rome, Addis Ababa, Kampala, Dar es Salaam, Kumasi, and London.

NIINA POLLARI is the author of the poetry collection *Dead Horse* (Birds, LLC, 2015) and, with merritt k, the chapbook *Total Mood Killer* (Tiger Bee Press, 2017).

KRYSTAL A. SITAL was born in the Republic of Trinidad and Tobago, and moved to the United States in 1999. Her critically acclaimed debut memoir, *Secrets We Kept: Three Women of Trinidad*, traces the hidden trauma and fierce resilience of one Trinidadian family in a story of ambition and cruelty, endurance and love, and the bonds among women and between generations that help them find peace with the past. A PEN Award finalist and Hertog Fellow, she holds an MFA from Hunter

College. Her work has appeared in *Elle*, *The New York Times Magazine*, *Salon*, *The New York Times* Well section, *Today's Parent*, *Catapult*, *The Margins*, *Literary Hub*, *The Caribbean Writer*, *Brain Child*, and elsewhere. Sital has taught creative writing; gender, sexuality, and culture; and peoples and cultures of the Caribbean at New Jersey City University and Fairleigh Dickinson University in New Jersey. She now teaches in the MFA program at Sierra Nevada College in Lake Tahoe. Sital lives in New Jersey with her partner and their three tiny humans.

NATALIA SYLVESTER is the author of the novels *Chasing the Sun*, which was named the Best Debut Book of 2014 by Latinidad; *Everyone Knows You Go Home*, which won an International Latino Book Award and received the 2019 Jesse H. Jones Award for Best Work of Fiction from the Texas Institute of Letters; and, most recently, *Running*, her debut YA novel published by Clarion Books/HMH. Sylvester's essays have appeared in *Bustle*, *Catapult*, *Electric Literature*, *Latina*, and *McSweeney's Publishing*.

SHARINE TAYLOR is a Toronto-based music and culture writer and critic, editor in chief and publisher of *BASHY Magazine*, a quarterly print and digital publication made for and by Jamaica and its diaspora. She is a *Vice* editorial intern alumna, the current Magazines Canada fellow fulfilling her term at *Azure Magazines*, and her bylines have appeared in *Dazed*, *Catapult*, *Hazlitt*, *The FADER*, *Noisey*, *Nylon*, *Vice*, and *Shondaland*. Her breadth of knowledge has given her opportunities to be a featured panelist at the Art Gallery of Ontario, Canadian Music Week, and at Sony Music (Canada). She's been a moderator for *Nuit Blanche*, a guest on CBC's *The Current*, in addition to having other opportunities to speak about Black, Jamaican, and/or Caribbean cultural production and identity.

KENECHI UZOR teaches writing at the University of Utah, where he is completing an MFA in creative writing. His work has appeared in *Electric Literature*, *Catapult*, *The Millions*, *Maple Tree Literary Supplement*, *Blue Monday Review*, *Brittle Paper*, *Afridiaspora*, *Saraba*, and other publications.

STEPH WONG KEN grew up in Miami and is currently based in Canada. Her work has appeared or is forthcoming in *Ninth Letter*, *Moss: A Journal of the Pacific Northwest*, *Joyland*, *Pithead Chapel*, and the *Cosmonauts Avenue Anthology*.

About the Editors

NICOLE CHUNG is the editor in chief of *Catapult* magazine and the author of *All You Can Ever Know.*

MENSAH DEMARY is a founding editor of *Catapult* magazine and editor at large of Catapult books and cowrote, with Common, the *New York Times* bestselling book *Let Love Have the Last Word.*